BRIDGING

WORLDS

By

SHAWN C. BURNETT

SHAWN C. BURNETT

Copyright © 2024

All Rights Reserved

Dedication

To my dear friend Ms. Vanessa Scott, for constantly reminding me for the last eight years to finish what I started.

Acknowledgment

I would like to extend my sincere thanks to the amazing team at "Amazon Publishing Direct," for keeping my lightbulb from dimming during my most difficult moments of creating. My beautiful wife for reminding me to not allow anyone to derail me from my path. I must also thank my family and friends who took the time to read my drafts and share their feedback with me. A special thank you to two awesome people who inspired this creative body of work; my daughter, Naliveeia, and my son, (Lil) Shawn. Without the love, guidance, and support of all of you, none of this would have been possible.

Disclaimer

Warning

This book contains violence that may be disturbing to some readers. Reader discretion is advised.

Contents

About the Author

Shawn Burnett is a writer with a passion for exploring the nuances in cultural behavior. Born and raised in Newark, New Jersey, Shawn Burnett's inspiration comes from a reflection of the good times he experienced while growing up in one of the most dangerous cities in America.

Although this is Shawn Burnett's very first novel, it already represents the culmination of his love for storytelling as well as his dedication to crafting authentic, thought-provoking narratives.

When not writing, Shawn Burnett can be found spending time at home with his family, exercising or having a drink or two with a close friend or relative (sometimes in that order), but mostly working long hours to provide a decent life for his family.

Shawn Burnett hopes that this book will resonate with readers and spark meaningful dialogue between parents who struggle to put their differences aside for the sake of their children. Connect with Shawn Burnett at shawncburnett@gmail.com to learn more about his writing journey and upcoming projects.

Foreword to "Bridging Worlds"

By: Christopher Randall

This life—this life generally, and Black male life specifically—is built on a cruciform existence marked by the perpetuation of myriad sufferings. When looked upon collectively and accurately, these sufferings will fortify us against and prepare us to handle the inescapable, deeply unavoidable vicissitudes of life. Deep and sincere sufferings, while they wound the spirit and pierce the heart, also become for some of us the fuel to propel us to provide unimagined levels of love and greatness, moving us toward lives that stand as monuments to the accuracy of the old adage 'what doesn't kill you makes you stronger.'

The pages of this blood-stained offering will allow readers to peer into the window of a life navigating the pitfalls marked by the ubiquity of systemic racism and oppression, anti-Black misandry, and all the perils that marginalization can provide. But that is not all that is available in these pages. Those who peruse this work will also experience the story of one who harnesses the best of the ancestral tradition bequeathed to them to provide a life that honors the realities of their pain but speaks to the glories that can be manifest in us all.

The pages of this text make clear, with a combination of pinpoint accuracy and piercing honesty, that each of us is more than the sum of our mistakes, misgivings, and misfortunes. Through the illumination of a singular life, inclusive of the belief in a liberating God, informed by a forging toward a more just existence, paternal and maternal commitment, as well as an unyielding devotion to greatness, we will see what we love in each of us. But we shall also see the parts of ourselves that horrify us. The truth is we are all a little 'Cole,' and 'Cole' is all a part of us. Enjoy this journey but continue on your path.

Chapter 1:

Beginnings:

A Tale of Two Worlds

The evening enveloped Passaic, New Jersey, in a chilly embrace, the wind whispering through the streets as autumn tightened its grip. Cole Anderson navigated his way through the sluggish traffic, the occasional drag of his cigarette punctuating the quiet of his ride. On the sidewalks, life painted its own vignettes. A young black woman with captivating curves pushed a stroller, her strides deliberate, her eyes rolling in response to the persistent attempts of some corner-bound homeboys trying to catch her attention with their rhymes.

Meanwhile, a skirmish brewed among a group of young Black and Latino men on a basketball court. Amidst their dispute over a call, a toddler, barely two, attempted an innocent dash onto the court, swiftly intercepted by his vigilant mother. Cole's car crawled ahead, eventually finding its parking haven. With a flick, he tossed the cigarette butt away, stepping out to retrieve groceries from the back of his 1995 Honda Accord. The distant wail of sirens pierced the air, swiftly followed by speeding cop cars careening down the street.

Crossing the road, Cole made his way into the apartment building, a familiar symphony greeting him with each step. The cacophony of a blaring television mingled with the plaintive cries of a baby, serenading him as he ascended the stairs. Dodging a rogue soccer ball that almost dislodged his grocery bags, he maintained his composure, traversing the lengthy hallway toward his sanctuary. Inside his home, the atmosphere carried its usual undertones. "Teesh!" Cole announced, depositing the bags on the kitchen table. "I got you those Teddy Bear crackers you nearly beheaded me for last time," he muttered to himself, the memory of Teesha's playful threat etched vividly in his mind.

Moving through the apartment, Cole called out to his partner, the pregnant Leticia, whom he lovingly called Teesh, due any day now. "Hey, baby, I got your crackers. You back there?" he inquired, the cool evening draft nudging at his consciousness. "It's getting cold out there too." Entering their bedroom, Cole found Teesha seated on the edge of their bed, the cordless house phone cradled in her hands. The weight of the imminent arrival of their child lingered palpably in the air, a quiet anticipation weaving between them.

"Teesh, everything okay?" Cole's concern laced his words as he approached her, his eyes locked onto her, seeking reassurance in the midst of their everyday routine. The charged atmosphere in the room crackled with uneasy tension as Leticia's voice sliced through the air, heavy with accusation and frustration. "Cole? Why the fuck are you and this bitch..." She paused, taking a deep breath to steady herself. "What do you and your baby mama be chatting about? Seventeen whole minutes on the phone that I pay for? Like, what could y'all really be talking about for a two-year-old?"

Cole, visibly taken aback by her sudden outburst, tried to diffuse the mounting tension. "Really? I wouldn't even speak to that girl if it weren't for my daughter. I don't know why you are tripping," he responded, his tone tinged with sarcasm. "Since you are doing phone checks, FYI, most of the time, I was listening to my baby girl. She kept saying, 'I luh Dada.' She sounded mad cute. I wish you could've heard her..." Leticia waved a dismissive hand, storming out of the room in disgust. Cole, trying to bridge the gap, followed her into the kitchen at a slower pace. "Babe, seriously, you need to chill, especially while you got my little man in the oven. I don't need him coming out crazy," he teased, attempting to lighten the mood, gently rubbing her stomach.

"Fumando," Leticia exclaimed, fanning her hand in front of her nose. "I hope you weren't smoking in my car," she remarked, arching an eyebrow skeptically. "Nah," Cole replied, shaking his head, denying the accusation. "And I'm not crazy. It's my hormones. I'd be happy when this little alien is out of me," Leticia retorted, a hint of humor peeking through her irritation.

"Yeah, I bet," Cole said, a playful grin dancing on his lips as Leticia handed him a bottle of mouthwash. "You thought it was cute when he first started kicking, and now he is kicking that ass." "Shut up," Leticia shot back, though a hint of amusement glinted in her eyes.

"Babe," Cole interjected, his tone softening, "You worked your entire pregnancy and finished school. You got this." Leticia's expression softened, a glimmer of vulnerability in her eyes. "What if I don't? You gonna carry him the next couple of weeks for me?" she teased, a hint of mischief lacing her words. Cole's laughter erupted as he spat out the mouthwash, the momentary tension dissipating. "I got your back and all, but I don't know about all that," he chuckled, shaking his head.

"Yeah, that's what I thought," Leticia quipped, a playful smile curving her lips as their laughter intertwined. Their banter eased into a moment of affection as the two leaned in, sharing a kiss, the silent promise of support and unity lingering between them. Cole, breaking the brief silence, teased playfully, "Umhmm. You wanna know the best thing about you being pregnant?"

Leticia, flirting back, raised an eyebrow. "What's that?" Cole's hands found their mark, playfully grabbing Leticia's bosom. "This badonkadonk came with it," he teased, his grin widening as they shared a mischievous moment together.

Leticia's fingers dug into Cole's calloused hands, her thumbs tracing the crescent scars from the long hours working under the oppressive sun. A mischievous glint sparked in her eyes, "Yeah, papi, you like it? Well, my hormones also got me extremely horny. Plus, the doctor encourages us to get it in a little more if we want the baby to come out easily. You got some work to attend to for the next couple of weeks." Cole's grin stretched wide, revealing teeth bleached by the same sun that bronzed his skin. "Word up, Doc said that? I knew I liked him!" He pumped his fist, a low chuckle rumbling in his chest. "Doctor's orders, right?"

Leticia squeezed his hand, savoring the rough warmth seeping through her skin. "Ooh, grande," she teased, her voice husky with unspoken desires. "I see you have a PhD, too." Her gaze drifted down, noting the faded outline of a scorpion tattooed on his wrist, a silent testament to hoodlum archives spent wrestling shadows.

A blush climbed Cole's neck, staining his sun-kissed cheeks. He mumbled, "Yeah, it's called a 'Pretty Hard Di…,' well you know what it is. But in all seriousness, I've been a little worried lately. Gotta spend some quality time with my own thoughts, rediscover what my heart and passion is, not just for me, but for us, feel me?" Leticia's playful smile softened. She traced the edge of his calloused knuckles, the touch sending shivers down her spine. "And what is your heart and passion saying right now, Cole?" she breathed, her voice barely a whisper against the heat that crackled between them.

Cole's gaze caught hers, locking her in a silent conversation. He pulled her closer, his breath mingling with hers. "My heart… well, my heart says it's tired of lonely sunsets and silent sunrises. It says it craves the warmth of another soul, the rhythm of two hearts, well, in this case, three hearts beating in unison. My passion is telling me to give into my desires and take what's mines."

His words sent a tremor through Leticia. Every nerve ending hummed with the electricity of possibility. For the first time in a while, the silence within her had found a voice. A melody echoed in the depths of Cole's gaze. With a sigh that sounded like desert wind through dry brush, she leaned in, the taste of salt and sun on his lips intoxicating. His kiss was like a desert rainstorm, sudden and fierce, washing away the essence of fear and leaving behind the fertile promise of new beginnings.

The world around them faded, echoing the darkness that bloomed behind their closed eyelids. It was a darkness painted with starlight, a darkness heavy with the sweet ache of unspoken desires and the whispered promise of a love forged in the heart of their offspring.

Chapter 2:
Fractured Lives

Cole's hurried footsteps echoed through the spacious yet tense atmosphere of his home. The morning light filtered in, casting a gentle glow on the room where Leticia cradled their newborn son, engaged in the tender act of breastfeeding. But this moment of familial intimacy was about to be overshadowed by an impending storm of emotions. "Good morning, baby one, baby two," Cole greeted affectionately, leaning in to kiss his son before addressing Leticia. "Hey, little man, save me some, okay? Teesh, everything good? I'm about to be out."

"Yeah... No, Cole, wait. There's something I've been wanting to know," Leticia's voice quivered with an underlying tension, her gaze fixed on Cole. "What's up? Make it quick, baby. I'm running late," Cole replied, his tone rushed, a hint of impatience underlying his words.

"I'm sorry, but this has been really bothering me, and I need to know," Leticia persisted, her words weighted with concern. "What's up?" Cole's eyebrows furrowed, confused by the sudden intensity of the conversation.

"Did you purposely miss the birth of your son because you weren't there for your daughter?" Leticia's words hung heavy in the air, abounded with accusation and hurt. "What? Teesh, how do you come up with this shit? I told you traffic was crazy on the bridge that day," Cole retorted, attempting to deflect the gravity of Leticia's inquiry with a touch of humor. "What? You wanted me to teleport to the hospital or something?"

The tension thickened, palpable in the charged silence that followed. Leticia's eyes bore into Cole's, searching for a truth that seemed elusive. "I'm not laughing, Cole! I know how you feel about your daughter. I know that you'll never love my son as much as you love her because she's your first!" Leticia's voice trembled with a mix of anguish and accusation, her vulnerability laid bare.

Cole scoffed. "Your son? Listen, Teesh, I ain't even tryna do this right now with you. You have been tripping ever since you had the baby," Cole's frustration simmered beneath the surface, his tone defensive. "Then don't! Matter of fact, you can get the fuck out! I'm tired of playing house with someone else's child!" Leticia's voice cracked with a rawness that echoed the fracture in their relationship.

"Whatever, we'll deal with this shit later," Cole's words spat out in an attempt to end the confrontation. "No, I want you out, now! Go be with that hood rat bitch and bastard child of yours!" Leticia's anger flared, her pain morphing into rage. Cole's eyes hardened, a storm brewing within as he glared at Leticia. Their gazes locked in a clash of emotions and unspoken words. Leticia, filled with a mixture of hurt and fury, gently placed the baby in the crib, her heart heavy with the weight of shattered trust and fractured bonds. The room felt charged, heavy with emotions that lingered, unresolved, leaving a palpable rift in their once-shared space.

The air crackled with tension, an explosive mixture of hurt, anger, and despair enveloping Cole and Leticia. Wounded by the verbal assault on his first born, Cole takes an aggressive leap towards Leticia. "What did you say about my daughter?" A retaliated slap echoed through the room, a resounding crack that shattered whatever fragile peace lingered between them. "Bitch, don't ever speak my daughter's name! And that's the only time I'm a let you slide putting your hands on me!" Cole's voice sliced through the charged atmosphere, his hand instinctively cupping his stinging jaw. His eyes blazed with a mixture of disbelief and indignation, his anger pulsating beneath the surface.

Leticia stood defiant, her hand still lingering in the air from the force of the slap. "You heard me! Yeah, now what? You gonna hit me?" Her words were sharp, laced with a mix of defiance and vulnerability. Cole's fists clenched at his sides, his body tensing as he took a step forward toward Leticia, a tempest brewing within him. The room seemed to shrink as their conflict escalated, the air thick with unspoken words and unbridled emotions.

"Yeah, I bet you'll like that," Cole retorted bitterly, his words dripping with disdain. "I'll pack my shit after work, don't worry." "No! Pack your shit now! I don't want you here!" Leticia's voice rose, a crescendo of anguish and fury.

The baby's cries pierced the escalating argument, a haunting reminder of innocence caught in the midst of their tumultuous exchange. But their tumult was deafening, drowning out all else, a tempestuous symphony of broken trust and unresolved pain.

*****

The heated exchange between Cole and Leticia reached a fever pitch, a tempest raging within the confines of their home. Each word uttered was a dagger, cutting deep into wounds neither knew how to heal. Amid the storm of their voices, a persistent pounding from the downstairs neighbor reverberated through the ceiling, an urgent plea for the turmoil to subside. Objects became projectiles in the midst of their verbal warfare, a manifestation of their inner turmoil given physical form. Vases shattered against walls, their fragile contents scattered like the shattered remnants of their fractured relationship. The room quaked with the sound of slamming doors and the cacophony of crashing items, each impact an echo of the tumultuous emotions that threatened to consume them.

In the midst of this chaotic symphony, Cole momentarily diverted his focus to a portrait hanging serenely in the hallway. Once a symbol of stability and family unity, now swayed precariously, an unintended casualty of the escalating toil. The framed image trembled on the wall, teetering on the brink of collapse as if mirroring the precarious state of their once-solid foundation.

With a final, decisive shudder, the portrait succumbed to the chaos, crashing to the ground with a resounding thud. The frame shattered on impact, scattering shards of glass like the fragmented pieces of their shattered life. The reverberating clatter served as a haunting punctuation mark to the discord that had engulfed their sanctuary, an ominous sign of the irreversible damage inflicted upon their shared history.

As the room continued to reverberate with the aftermath of their confrontation, the fallen portrait lay amidst the debris—a poignant symbol of the shattered dreams, broken promises, and irreparable wounds that now defined their fractured existence. Its descent marked the culmination of their unraveling, a grim testament to the depth of their despair.

The argument faded, the cacophony dulled, and the turmoil transcended into a haunting silence—a poignant representation of the shattered echoes resonating in the wake of their explosive confrontation.

Chapter 3:

Crossroads

The scorching sun bore down on Kennedy Towers in the heart of Newark's South Ward, enveloping the neighborhood in a sweltering embrace. It was a hot day in May, the kind that left the air heavy and oppressive, hanging like a thick blanket over the streets. Life unfolded in a kaleidoscope of simultaneous scenes, each one painting a stark portrait of the community's diverse struggles. As the sun blazed, the radio host's voice cut through the airwaves, a familiar soundtrack to the lives of those navigating the harsh realities of the neighborhood. His words were a blend of sports excitement and local flavor, promising a brief respite from the hardships that defined their daily existence.

In the streets below, the scenes unfolded in discordant harmony, a snapshot of the complex tapestry of life in Kennedy Towers. A young man skillfully dribbled his basketball, navigating through a litter-strewn path, his determined focus a stark contrast to the shattered glass and discarded drug paraphernalia beneath his feet. Meanwhile, a grim tableau unfolded in a small park, where two addicts battled over a seat, their desperation and need for a fix escalating into a violent struggle. The man's frantic gestures to prepare the drug punctuated the harsh reality of addiction that plagued the community.

Across the way, the innocence of childhood clashed with the harshness of reality as three giggling kids engaged in a playful water fight, their innocent joy tempered by the tears of the smallest girl, drenched and distressed amidst the laughter. Further down the street, a group of local street runners gathered, their hushed conversations punctuated by animated gestures, each one sharing stories of the urban jungle they navigated daily—a world where danger and excitement often walked hand in hand.

In one of the tower's windows, an old lady briefly observed the scene below, her gaze a mix of concern and resignation before she retreated, pulling the blinds shut and shielding herself from the harsh truths playing out outside her window. The streets hummed with a complex melody of life— hope clashing with despair, resilience battling against adversity, and dreams striving to rise above the suffocating heat of reality. Each scene was a testament to the intricate tapestry of human existence within the crucible of Kennedy Towers, where life unfolded in vivid and often heartbreaking hues.

In the cramped quarters of Tanashia Anderson's home, the morning bustled with a sense of urgency. Tanashia, affectionately called Nae Nae by her family, darted through the cluttered rooms of the small three-bedroom apartment. She was adorned in professional attire, a testament to her aspirations as she readied herself for a pivotal job interview.

"Mom!" Tanashia called out, her voice tinged with a sense of haste and responsibility. Tracy, her mother, emerged into the living room, casting a discerning eye over Tanashia's professional ensemble. With a deft hand, Tracy plucked a stray string from Tanashia's hair, a silent gesture of maternal care amidst the morning rush.

Tanashia hastily scoured the cluttered space, muttering about a missing earring, convinced of her sister Shannon's possible involvement. A quick lift of the bedspread from the couch revealed the elusive earring, prompting a relieved smile from Tanashia. "Don't forget to tell Damon to pick Shannon up from school!" Tanashia's reminder was a testament to the intricate family responsibilities she juggled alongside her aspirations.

Tracy nodded, acknowledging the reminder, then turned her attention to Tanashia's choice of shoes. A pair of Tracy's own shoes rested on Tanashia's feet, borrowed for the crucial interview, eliciting a teasing comment from Tracy about Tanashia's penchant for expensive sneakers. "See, now you need mine because you be wasting your money on those expensive, ugly ass 'J's' and 'KB's,'" Tracy chided, referring to the pricey sneakers Tanashia favored. Their banter, a familiar exchange, held an undercurrent of concern for Tanashia's financial choices.

Tanashia's stature exuded a quiet confidence, her posture straight and purposeful as she moved with a grace that belied the chaos of her surroundings. Though her clothing was simple, tailored to fit her form, there was an undeniable elegance to her presence that commanded attention.

Her eyes, a deep shade of mahogany, held a depth of emotion that spoke volumes of the challenges she had faced and overcome. There was a fire within them, a fierce determination to carve out a better future for herself and her family, no matter the obstacles in her path.

Tanashia, unfazed by the gentle reprimand, acknowledged her mother's words and promised to return the borrowed shoes in pristine condition. Tracy's wishes for Tanashia's success held a sense of hope not just for her daughter's future but for the family's collective well-being. "Okay, Mom, I gotta go. This place is like an hour away, and you know how the buses are running," Tanashia hurriedly stated, conscious of the time ticking away.

Tracy's maternal instinct urged Tanashia on, reminding her not to dawdle as she dashed out of the door. Their hurried exchange ended with a tight embrace, a silent reassurance between mother and daughter. As Tanashia sprinted up the street towards the bus stop, Tracy called out her final words of encouragement, her voice carrying a mix of concern and love for her daughter. Tanashia, already halfway down the street, acknowledged her mother's good wishes before disappearing out of sight.

"And good luck, baby, and make sure you call me when you're done!" Tracy's words echoed down the street, a reminder of her unwavering support for Tanashia's endeavors.

Amidst the backdrop of their modest home and the bustling neighborhood, Tanashia's aspirations soared against the weight of their shared struggles, with Tracy's love and hope accompanying her on this crucial step toward a brighter future.

*****

On the bus ride to her job appointment, Tanashia sat in contemplation, the weight of anticipation and anxiety pulling at her thoughts. Her mind oscillated between hopeful anticipation for the job opportunity and the worry of being slightly behind schedule. As her phone buzzed with a text notification, Tanashia's thoughts were interrupted. She glanced at the screen to see a message from her father, a gesture of encouragement that brought a smile to her face amid the flurry of nerves.

"Good luck today, honey," the message read, followed by a series of light-hearted exchanges between Tanashia and her dad, a brief reprieve from the mounting tension. Despite the slight delay and the banter with her father, Tanashia's focus sharpened as the bus approached her stop. Pulling herself together, she checked the time on her phone, swiftly pocketed it, and made her way off the bus, determined not to let the delay derail her aspirations.

Arriving at United Transit HQ, Tanashia approached the reception desk, her demeanor poised despite the slight lateness. However, her attempt at explanation was met with brusque rudeness from the receptionist, a dismissive attitude that instantly soured the atmosphere. The receptionist's sharp retorts stung Tanashia, whose attempts to explain the delay were repeatedly interrupted, amplifying the tension in the already charged interaction. The supervisor, a composed figure in the midst of the escalating confrontation, intervened, diffusing the situation with her calm demeanor.

"Hello, Ms. Sandra, who do we have here?" the supervisor inquired, redirecting the attention away from the receptionist's curt behavior. Undeterred by the initial friction,

Tanashia introduced herself and explained her purpose, grateful for the supervisor's understanding tone. The supervisor's gesture of empathy and willingness to provide a grace period softened the edges of Tanashia's anxiety, offering a glimmer of hope in an otherwise tense moment.

With a gracious nod from the supervisor, Tanashia moved past the reception area, shooting a disdainful glance at the uncooperative receptionist. The exchange left an acrid taste in the air, a clash of personalities and attitudes that lingered as Tanashia headed toward the next room.

As she found her seat, Tanashia reflected on the encounter. Despite the rocky start, the supervisor's understanding renewed her confidence. With a renewed determination, Tanashia prepared herself to seize the opportunity, ready to face whatever challenges lay ahead in her pursuit of a better future.

*****

Seated in the quiet testing room, Tanashia's gaze drifted from the examination booklet to the diverse array of individuals surrounding her, all vying for the same opportunity. Her eyes flitted over the faces, each person a testament to the shared desire for a chance at a better future. Focusing on the test before her, Tanashia delved into the questions, her mind absorbed in the task at hand. But amidst the silence and concentration, a sudden flashback pulled her away from the present, transporting her to a different time and place.

In the flashback, a young Tanashia, merely eight years old, sat in a classroom much like the testing room she occupies now. The scene unfolded with familiar chaos—students chattering, laughter filling the air, and the occasional disruption drawing the teacher's attention. The teacher's attempts to maintain order echoed in the classroom, a small urban setting bustling with the energy of the students. Amidst the commotion, Tanashia's attention was drawn to the task at hand—the assignment to use specific words correctly in sentences.

As the flashback zoomed in on the word "Departed," Tanashia found herself drawn away from the task, her mind wandering to a small, cherished photo of her and her younger brother, Aaron, a treasured memory from years past.

The ringing of the bell jolted Tanashia back to the present, abruptly ending the flashback and pulling her away from the reminiscence of simpler times. Exiting the testing site, Tanashia found herself waiting for her ride, a quiet calm settling within her. The echoes of the past reverberated in her thoughts, intertwining with the aspirations she held for her future.

As she stood in the present, her heart heavy with the weight of memories and aspirations, Tanashia harbored a sense of determination—a resolve to overcome obstacles and grasp the opportunity that lay before her, echoing the aspirations of that young girl in the classroom years ago.

Chapter 4:

A Heartrending Reunion

The car ride was cloaked in darkness, the evening sky matching the somber atmosphere within the vehicle. Tanashia sat, her frustration palpable in the confined space, her words simmering with an undertone of disappointment and anger. "I can't understand how it's so easy for you to just forget about me and keep me waiting like that!" Tanashia's voice carried a blend of hurt and irritation, her disappointment evident.

Beside her, Whiz exuded a nonchalant energy, his demeanor markedly different from Tanashia's charged emotions. He appeared indifferent, his careless attitude highlighted by the minor cuts and bruises on his face, a physical testament to his reckless behavior. Whiz, with an air of unconcern, offered Tanashia a distraction in the form of a blunt. However, Tanashia's refusal and mounting frustration only seemed to exacerbate the tension between them.

"You serious? You left me out here stranded in the middle of nowhere for mad long, and you expect me not to be upset?" Tanashia's words dripped with indignation and hurt, her gestures punctuating her exasperation. Their exchange escalated, each word another notch in the rising tension. Whiz, seemingly unaffected by Tanashia's anger, nonchalantly steered the conversation into a lighthearted tease, attempting to defuse the situation with a casual demeanor.

As the car pulled over, a fleeting moment of panic flashed in Tanashia's eyes when Whiz toyed with the idea of leaving her stranded. His attempt at a joke fell flat, the lines between playful banter and genuine frustration blurring in the confined space. Their verbal jousting escalated, punctuated by a silence that spoke volumes. The weight of unspoken words hung heavy in the air, a palpable tension that reverberated between them.

"I'm good. Just take me home," Tanashia's terse request held a hint of weariness, her patience worn thin by the escalating confrontation. "A 'please' would be nice," Whiz retorted, a hint of annoyance tainting his tone. Silence lingered, an unspoken standoff as the car continued its journey, both passengers engulfed in their own thoughts. The night enveloped them, cloaking the strained atmosphere in an eerie quietude, leaving the unspoken grievances to linger in the darkness.

The air hung heavy with unresolved tension as Tanashia sat in the car, her emotions simmering beneath a thin veneer of silent restraint. Whiz's attempts to lighten the mood fell flat, his casual dismissal of Tanashia's frustration only adding to her sense of isolation. "Damn, yo, you really heated. I got you next time, a'ight?" Whiz's laughter grated on Tanashia's already frayed nerves, his nonchalant demeanor amplifying her feelings of being unheard and disregarded.

As Tanashia turned away, her gaze fixed on the passing scenery outside the car window, she erected an emotional barrier, a silent protest against Whiz's dismissive behavior. A solitary tear trickled down her cheek, a silent testament to the turmoil brewing within. Their journey came to a halt outside the projects where Tanashia lived, the flickering streetlights casting an eerie glow over the desolate surroundings. Whiz's demeanor shifted, his casual tone belying an underlying threat as he inquired about Tanashia's brother, hinting at a peace offering while brandishing a gun.

"Can I get a kiss?" Whiz's demand hung in the air, met with Tanashia's cold indifference. She offered him her cheek, a deliberate refusal to engage in his antics, her silent rejection emblematic of the emotional chasm between them. Whiz's menacing smile contrasted with Tanashia's stoic farewell. As she exited the car and slammed the door shut, Whiz's smirk remained, his expression betraying a sense of dominance and control as he drove off into the night.

Alone in the silence of the night, Tanashia felt the weight of the unresolved conflict bearing down on her. The shadowy presence of Whiz's veiled threats lingered, leaving her grappling with a mix of fear, frustration, and a sense of unease for what the future might hold. As she made her way toward her home, the darkness enveloping her echoed the turmoil within, a haunting reminder of the complex and uneasy reality she navigated.

*****

As the evening draped the neighborhood in fading light, Tanashia strolled through the familiar streets of Kennedy Towers, where the cacophony of urban life formed the backdrop to her evening. Amidst the commotion—dogs barking, a car alarm blaring, and the distressing plea of a homeless man—Tanashia navigated the bustling streets, averse to the approaching figure. The unwelcome advances dissolved into laughter as a familiar voice emerged from the shadows.

"Damn boo, you fine as hell. Bring that little dirty ass over here!" The man's audacious approach was met with Tanashia's defiant stance, her retort laced with playful defiance. It was Cooley, a close friend, who pulled Tanashia into the sanctuary of a small alleyway, their camaraderie palpable amidst the evening's chaos. Cooley's demeanor shifted from masculine bravado to feminine banter, offering a reprieve from the day's tribulations.

"What you gonna do with them little hands? You tryna massage a bitch?" Cooley teased. Their playful banter was a familiar comfort in the midst of Tanashia's frustrations.

"Well, sweetheart, you said you'll be back like six, and it's way past six. What, you stopped at a happy hour or something?" Cooley's smooth, streetwise tone carried a hint of playful banter as he intercepted Tanashia's path.

"Two hours late picking me up, this fool." Tanashia's frustration seeped into her words, accompanied by an eye roll. "Had me standing out there, catching stares from every direction. White guys eyeing me like I was up for grabs." Cooley's eyes swept over Tanashia, appreciating her presence. "Gotta say, boo, you are looking mighty scrumptious."

A sly smile played on Tanashia's lips. "Well, they gotta pay up if they want a taste." "I hear that," Cooley nodded, understanding the game. "But Whiz ain't right for that, though. Why are you still dealing with him and his crusty-lip self?" Tanashia chuckled. "Cooley, you're too much. He's just going through a lot right now." "Yeah, a lot of drinking, smoking, talking shit, and getting his ass kicked for it," Cooley retorted. "Too bad you ain't my type, or I'd have snatched you away from him myself. Speaking of which, how's your fine-ass gangsta brother?"

Tanashia lowered her voice, leaning closer. "Cooley, you better stop it. You know my brother won't take kindly to you checking him out." Cooley grinned mischievously. "Ooh, girl, don't threaten me with a good time. You know I like it rough. So, what's the plan, heffa? Are we turning up or what?"

Sharing snippets of her day, Tanashia confided in Cooley about the lengthy job test and Whiz's tardiness, the incident rife with irritation and latent disappointment. Cooley's witty remarks and unwavering support provided a welcome respite, their banter filled with shared understanding and inside jokes.

Their conversation meandered, Cooley's sassy commentary drawing laughter from Tanashia, momentarily lightening the weight of the evening's grievances. Yet beneath the banter, Cooley expressed concern for Tanashia's involvement with Whiz, punctuating their exchange with humorous yet pointed observations. Their verbal sparring took a flirtatious turn as Cooley cheekily inquired about Tanashia's older brother, evoking a hushed warning from Tanashia. Their playful banter danced on the edge of audacity, a blend of camaraderie and teasing familiarity that characterized their friendship.

As the conversation shifted, Tanashia disclosed her plans to collect her sister, Shannon, from Kiki's house, emphasizing the responsibilities she shouldered in her household. Cooley's playful jibes and teasing remarks about Kiki brought a smile to Tanashia's face, their banter a temporary reprieve from the challenges of everyday life. The night enveloped them in its embrace, the alleyway a haven of shared laughter and candid conversations, offering a brief escape from the complexities of their lives. Amidst the laughter and teasing, their camaraderie remained a steadfast anchor in the unpredictable currents of their urban existence.

*****

In the fading light of the evening, Tanashia stood outside Kiki's door, a sense of familiarity enveloping her as she awaited entry into her brother's girlfriend's home. The sounds of urban life ebbed in the background, a muted symphony compared to the familial warmth she was about to step into. Shannon, Tanashia's ten-year-old sister, opened the door, her youthful enthusiasm evident as she greeted her elder sister.

"Where's Kiki?" Tanashia inquired, her concern for her brother's girlfriend palpable. "In her room, watching TV,"

Shannon replied, her innocence tinted with a touch of excitement at Tanashia's arrival.

As Tanashia entered the apartment, she engaged in a brief exchange with Shannon about her snack, chuckling softly at her sister's playful slang. The mundane interaction was a snapshot of their sibling dynamic—a blend of care and affection tinted with sibling banter. Approaching Kiki's room, Tanashia called out, "Key?" to which Kiki responded from within, signaling her presence while tending to her daily routine.

As Kiki exited the bathroom, the subtle sound of the running water tapered off. Tanashia's eyes met Kiki's, a silent acknowledgment passing between them, a shared understanding forged by the ties of family and shared experiences. Their interaction, while brief, carried an unspoken depth—an unbreakable bond that transcended mere acquaintanceship. As Kiki stood before Tanashia, a sense of ease and comfort emanated from their unspoken connection, a testament to the familial unity they shared.

Chapter 5:

Echoes

In the cozy familiarity of Kiki's living room, the soft glow of a table lamp illuminated the scene. Tanashia, perched on the arm of the sofa, peered at Kiki with concern. "Girl, you okay?" she inquired, her eyes reflecting genuine care.

Kiki reclined on the sofa cushions and offered a reassuring smile. "Yeah, boo. I'm good. How'd your appointment go?" Tanashia sighed, her demeanor shifting slightly. "It went okay. Just playing the 'waiting game' now." "Don't wait too long. You gotta stay on them," Kiki advised with a knowledgeable tone. "If you don't hear from them in like a week, start calling them. That's what my girl Tisha did. She's been working there for like two years now."

Tanashia nodded appreciatively. "Yeah, I definitely will. Are you sure you are okay? I can run back out and get you something before the store closes." "No, no, I'm fine, baby, thanks. Just waiting for Damon to come in, and then I'm gonna take it down," Kiki assured her, a hint of anticipation in her voice.

"Okay, let me get her home. She ain't give you no trouble, right?" Kiki chuckled, shaking her head. "Girl, you know she good here." "You know I gotta ask. It's the first thing mom asks me," Tanashia replied, a playful glint in her eye. "Well, let my brother know we're home, and I'm going a hook him for eating my chicken last night. Now I gotta settle for Ramen Noodles and sardines."

Kiki laughed, understanding the sibling dynamics. "Girl, you know you gotta hide food when he's around." "Uh-huh, his greedy behind self. Alright, Key, I'll see you later."

"Bye-bye, Auntie Kiki," Shannon chimed in, offering a small wave. "Okay, bye ladies, text me when y'all get in," Kiki called after them, directing a teasing remark to Shannon, "You too, chipmunk."

*****

In the quiet sanctuary of Shannon's room, Tanashia tenderly tucked her sister into bed. Soft lamplight casts a warm glow, creating a comforting atmosphere. "You brushed your teeth while you were in the bathroom, right?" Tanashia inquired, her tone a playful blend of skepticism and affection. Shannon giggled in response, her eyes sparkling with innocence.

"I don't believe you. Let me smell for stink-bots," Tanashia teased, her fingers dancing over Shannon's sides, eliciting laughter. "Okay, I believe you. It smells nice and minty. Ok, goodnight, little bit." As Tanashia pulled the covers snugly around Shannon, the young girl, inquisitive as ever, piped up, "Is Aunty Kiki gonna be okay?"

Surprised by the unexpected concern, Tanashia paused before responding. "Yeah, why do you ask that?" Shannon, her voice filled with empathy, shared her observations, "She was sick and throwing up all day, and any time she tried to eat, she threw it up, and I think it made her sad because she was crying."

Tanashia hesitated for a moment, her maternal instincts guiding her response. "Yes, sweetheart, she'll be fine." She bent down to place a gentle kiss on Shannon's cheek. "Goodnight."

Exiting Shannon's room, Tanashia retreated into her own space. The room felt cozy and familiar as she settled into her bed. A contented smile graced her face as she contemplated the possibility that her brother, Damon, might soon become a father.

*****

Under the evening lights, the high school baseball stadium stood as a battleground, the air thick with the tension of the conference finals. Coach Ebbers, a figure of authority and inspiration, gathered his players in the dugout, a rallying cry echoing through the confines.

"You guys are ten innings away from being champions. Think about how far you all have come and how hard you guys worked to get here," Coach Ebbers emphasized, his words cutting through the nervous energy. "Remember that they had to work their asses off to get here, too, which is exactly why you guys all have to be 'the very best' at what you do. Bring everything you worked hard for to the field and leave it there. This is our game! Let's go take it! Let's kick some ass! Spartans on three. 1! 2! 3! Spartans!"

On the field, the opponents reveled in a recent two-point advantage, the pitcher poised with confidence, ready to secure the win. Karl Jacobs, a fleet-footed player, stepped up to the plate. The first pitch, a formidable 82mph fastball, whizzed past him, earning a resounding "Strike!" from the umpire. Locked in, Jacobs braced for the next delivery. The second pitch, a deceptive slider, found contact with Jacobs' bat, resulting in a mid-field pop-up and one out for the Spartans.

Coach Ebbers, undeterred by the setback, turned his attention to the next batter. "Ok, Cato, I need you to get on base. Go get 'em, son."

Doug Cato approached the plate, determined and confident. The pitcher, eyeing victory with only two outs left, unleashed a fireball. Cato's swing connected, sending the ball soaring into the right side of the outfield. The crowd erupted as the ball cleared the park, and Cato rounded the bases for a triumphant home run.

"Alright, Anderson, you're up. You know what you gotta do. Get out there and show them something," Coach Ebbers encouraged, the team rallying behind their designated hitter.

Aaron Anderson stepped into the batter's box, the crowd hushing as anticipation settled over the stadium. The pitcher, visibly rattled, sought guidance from the catcher. The first pitch, a blazing fastball, zipped past Anderson for a called strike. Undeterred, Anderson refocused for the next pitch – a merciless slider that left him swinging at thin air.

Now fired up and sensing the gravity of the moment, Aaron geared up for the next pitch. The crack of the bat echoed through the stadium as Anderson connected with the ball, sending it toward the third baseman. Sprinting at full tilt, he made it to first just ahead of the throw, marked "Safe!" by the umpire.

The crowd roared with excitement, setting the stage for the next batter, Matt Cousy, a reliable hitter who had faced recent challenges at the plate. As the first pitch, a wicked slider, cut across the plate, Cousy froze.

"Strike!" declared the umpire, heightening the tension.

Cousy recalibrated for the next pitch – a fastball down the middle. The satisfying smack of the bat meeting ball sent it soaring to the back of the outfield. Anderson sprinted to second, the outfielder chasing down the ball. A swift throw to second ensued.

"Safe!" announced the umpire, marking a crucial advancement for the Spartans. The stadium echoed with cheers as the narrative of the game unfolded, each swing and catch shaping the destiny of the team.

Under the floodlights of the high school baseball stadium, the stakes hung heavy in the air. With two outs and down by a single point, Coach Ebbers's team found themselves at the precipice of victory or defeat. The mood was tense as the casual, nonchalant designated hitter, Caleb "Some-Timing" Sutton, stepped up to the plate. Known for his inconsistency in actual games despite being a practice superstar, Sutton was about to face a pivotal moment.

Coach Ebbers placed a reassuring hand on Sutton's shoulder, uncertainty flickering in his gaze as he spoke, "This is the big one, son. I hope you can prove these folks wrong about you. Good luck." Sutton responded with a dull smile, a trademark of his nonchalant demeanor, as he hustled over to home plate. Aaron Anderson waited patiently at second base, the team's hopes resting on the shoulders of the enigmatic DH. The crowd hushed, breaths held collectively, as the pitcher prepared for the first pitch—a fastball. Sutton swung with such force that he nearly toppled to the ground, missing the ball entirely.

Disbelief washed over the team, visible in their expressions, yet Sutton remained unfazed. He wiped himself down, picked up his bat, and cracked a defiant smile, injecting a glimmer of hope into the hearts of the spectators. The next pitch, a breaking ball, saw Sutton connecting but sending the ball flying into the crowd—a foul. Arrogantly, Sutton tucked his bat between his legs and began "raising the roof" to the crowd, sparking erratic cheers from his fans and frustration from the opposition. Locked in and ready, he faced the next pitch—a perfect slider. The crack of the bat echoed as Sutton sent the ball soaring over the first baseman's head, hobbling into the deep corner of the outfield. Anderson strolled in from second to home while Sutton sprinted from base to base.

Coaches shouted for Sutton to stay at third, anticipating the ball being launched toward the infield. But Sutton had bigger plans. Ignoring the cautionary calls, he sprinted through third, hurdling toward home plate. The umpire and back catcher awaited both the ball and Sutton's arrival. In an exhilarating crescendo, Sutton and the ball reached home plate simultaneously. A collision between Sutton and the back catcher ensued. "Safe!" declared the umpire, sealing the game. The stadium erupted in joy as the team celebrated their hard-fought victory.

As the players rejoiced amongst themselves, they gradually separated, connecting with their families and friends in the crowd. Aaron made his way toward his most prominent supporters: his mom, Leticia, his Aunty Jacqueline, and her six-year-old son, Tino.

"Good game, Jefe. You guys had me so nervous out here. I was like, 'Get them, Double A!' I said it right, right? Did I say it right?" Leticia exclaimed. "Yes, way to go, man!" Aunty Jacqueline added, applauding Aaron's remarkable performance. The echoes of victory and the warmth of familial pride filled the air as the team basked in the glory of their triumph.

Chapter 6:

Shadows of Turmoil

In the jubilant aftermath of the victorious baseball game, young Tino's excitement bubbled over as he addressed Aaron, his eyes wide with admiration. "I saw you hit the ball, Aaron! Can you teach me how to hit like that, please?" Tino's enthusiasm mirrored the infectious energy that still lingered in the air.

Leticia, Aaron's mom, chimed in, her pride evident in her words, "And Caleb with that game-ender! His mom would be so proud of him, such a good kid, just misunderstood." As the group continued their conversation, Leticia discreetly pointed further down the bleachers, urging Aaron to look in that direction. Squinting through the crowd, Aaron's gaze landed on a familiar face—his dad. A surge of joy lit up Aaron's face as he high-stepped across the bleachers towards him.

"Dad, what's up? I thought you weren't going to make it. Have you been here the whole time? Why are you sitting alone down here? Did you see us?" Aaron's rapid-fire questions reflected his genuine surprise and curiosity. Cole, Aaron's dad, slowly stood up, a warm smile playing on his lips as he addressed his son, "Yes, yes, son. You guys played one hell of a game. I'm so proud of you."

Concern crept into Aaron's voice as he observed his father more closely. "Dad, are you okay?"

"Yeah, I stayed down here because I ain't want you to see me, then go get all nervous out there and stuff, you know?" Cole explained, attempting to downplay his own presence. Aaron, however, persisted, "No, Dad, you know what I mean. And what's the cane for?" Awash with paternal affection, Cole gently reassured his son, "Aw, son, don't worry about that. Go hit the showers, and I'll be waiting out back for you. While you're in there, figure out where we're going to celebrate this victory. Bring whoever you want, my treat."

Aaron, now wearing a more concerned expression, gazed down at his father, wrestling with the weight of the revelation about his physical condition. "A'ight, dad, see you in a few." With a lingering glance, he turned away, emotions swirling within him as he made his way to the locker room. The victory, though sweet, was now tinged with a newfound awareness of the challenges his father faced.

*****

The car buzzed with laughter as Master P's distinctive beats filled the air, a nostalgic throwback to Cole's earlier years. Cole, at the wheel, couldn't help but revel in the music, unleashing his inner hype man.

"Uhhh! Uhhh! Na-nah na-nah! Na-nah na nah! Lemme hear ya say Uhhh! Uhhh!" Cole belted out, grooving to the rhythm, glancing at his son, Aaron, and Caleb in the backseat. The boys erupted in laughter, finding amusement in Cole's exuberant display. "See y'all some young jokers, and y'all don't know nothin' bout that! That boy Master P had the game on lock when y'all were in diapers. Reminds me of my old runnin' days," Cole chuckled, turning down the music and sharing a nostalgic look around the car.

Aaron and Caleb couldn't contain their laughter, responding to Cole's antics with even more amusement. "Pops, if you don't get that old-school junk outta here! P couldn't rap, act, or play ball," Aaron teased, provoking another round of laughter. "He couldn't have been that bad with all the money he made, huh?" Cole retorted, glancing at Caleb, who nodded in agreement. "Hell, one of the richest rappers, still to this day. So whatchu' talkin' about?"

"Whatever, man. He could be rich, but he ain't relevant," Aaron quipped. "Shit, I'll rather be rich? Wouldn't you?" Cole responded, challenging Aaron's assertion.

Caleb chimed in, "I'm with Pops on this one, homie. Show me the dough!"

The banter continued as laughter reverberated within the car. Cole, grinning, playfully turned to Caleb, urging him to school Aaron. "Cay, you better school your boy." As they pulled up to a local restaurant, the camaraderie lingered, setting the stage for their continued celebration.

Inside the restaurant, the aroma of barbecue ribs wafted through the air as the trio settled into a booth. Laughter echoed through the establishment as Caleb raved about the mouthwatering ribs. "Man, them barbecue ribs was rocking!" Mocking one of their favorite movies, Caleb comically erupts, "Taste so good, make you wanna..." playfully takes a swing at Aaron, "slap yo brother! I'm trying to get a job here just so I can get them joints for free."

Amidst the lighthearted banter, Cole took a moment to express his pride in the boys. "Fellas, I just want to say again, 'Great game.' You guys played through adversity, being down in the ninth and not quitting. That's what real winners do," Cole commended, a fatherly pride evident in his voice. Turning to Caleb, he addressed the nickname circulating around him.

"Cay, you know I've heard what they say about you. They call you 'Some-Timing,' right?" Cole smirked, acknowledging Caleb's moniker. "Well, how about it? 'Some timing, right?'" He extended a fist for a pound, sealing the acknowledgment.

"Now what they gonna say?" Cole mused, raising his glass. "In fact, let's drink to that." He flagged down the waitress, ready to toast to the triumphs of the evening.

"Excuse me, sweetheart. Can you get us, um, let's see, three shots of Jack?" Cole requested, his eyes gleaming with the spirit of celebration. The night, filled with laughter, music, and camaraderie, continued to unfold as they embraced the victory and each other's company.

The waitress approached their booth, a friendly smile gracing her face as she greeted them. "Sure. Can I see y'all IDs?" she inquired, a routine part of her job.

Cole, ever the charmer, leaned back in his seat, a glint of pride in his eyes as he gestured toward his two boys. "Listen, honey, you see these two handsome fellas here, these my sons, and I don't know if you follow sports, but these two are doing it big for this city. In fact, they're heading to the biggest game this city has seen since the early '90s. So, if you can just take this," he smoothly slid a fifty-dollar bill across the table, "and you know, 'do your thing,' I'd greatly appreciate it. No change will be necessary, sweetheart."

The waitress, charmed by the gesture, couldn't help but smile. "Three Jacks are coming right up, sir." Caleb, amused by Cole's tactics, teased, "You sure have a way with the ladies, 'Dad.'" Aaron, with a hint of sarcasm, added, "Yeah, a real charmer." The boys shared a laugh at Cole's unconventional approach.

"Whatever. Y'all got y'all tricks," Cole retorted, rubbing his pointer fingers and thumbs together, "and I got mine."

Caleb, ever the observant one, couldn't resist poking fun at the situation. "Yeah, Mr. A., I'm guessing the cane is part of your tricks, too, because I just saw you about a week ago, and you were perfectly fine. That's low, Mr. A., tryna use that senior citizen swag. A real stunner, Mr. A."

Caleb's laughter echoed alone while Aaron posted a discerning look towards his father. Though Caleb played the fool, Aaron knew there was a deeper reason behind the cane. The waitress returned with their drinks, and Cole, ever the gentleman, thanked her, "Enjoy your drinks, guys."

"Thank you, sweetheart. You have a lovely evening," Cole replied, his eyes meeting hers with a flirtatious twinkle. As the waitress walked away, Cole seized the opportunity to impart some wisdom to his sons.

"Y'all see that? Something that'll never go out of style: chivalry and big tipping. Now grab your glasses, and don't be looking at me all silly and shit like it's y'all first drink because I know it ain't. I want to give a toast to you boys on your success, on and off the field, and for more to come. Now, let's go and get that trophy next week! Cheers!"

The boys raised their glasses in unison, responding with a hearty "Cheers!" The air was charged with a sense of celebration, familial bonds, and the shared anticipation of the victories yet to come.

*****

As Cole's car pulled up to Caleb's house, the trio exchanged parting words in the cool night air. "Thanks, Mr. A., for tonight," Caleb expressed his gratitude, turning to Aaron. "Ace, I'm going for a ride on my bike tomorrow."

"Get there early. Mom's making breakfast," Aaron replied with a grin.

"Oh yeah, no doubt, I can't miss those Magadillas," Caleb teased.

"'Magdalenas?'" Aaron corrected, amused.

"Yeah, that's what I said. A'ight, peace."

"Later."

As Cole and Aaron drove off, their camaraderie lingered in the air.

"That's a funny kid," Cole remarked, a smile playing on his lips.

"Yeah, he's a handful. I'm like the only one who gets him," Aaron confessed.

"That's because y'all are both crazy! But seriously, that's good, though, that you two remained friends over the years. A lot of people will come and go, but try to keep the good ones close," Cole advised a touch of wisdom in his words.

"So, dad, you gonna tell me what's going on with you?" Aaron inquired, turning the conversation to a more serious note.

"C'mon, have some faith in me. I'm almost eighteen. I can handle it."

Cole let out a deep sigh, his gaze fixed on the road. "Listen, son, I'm not exactly sure yet. The doctors overlooked some things, and I might've been misdiagnosed, but now they're reevaluating everything. I just want you to know despite what happens, you continue to be strong, stay focused on your education, and become a great man, a better one than me. I know I made some mistakes, but I also know that I made you, and you aren't a mistake – far from it. You make me proud, my boy…"

Aaron's face tightened as he fought back tears, the weight of his father's words sinking in. "You hear me son? I am proud of you." Hesitating, Aaron cleared his throat and managed a smile.

"A'ight! Just stop talking like you gon' croak or something." As Cole pulled up to Aaron's house, they exchanged their final words in the warm glow of the car's interior.

"Goodnight, son. Tell your mother I said goodnight as well. And don't mention to her the drink we shared, or else I'll really have a problem," Cole advised, both of them sharing a knowing smile.

"Alright, goodnight, Dad."

As Aaron stepped out of the car, the night embraced him with its calmness. Aaron's home was a quiet suburban haven, a significant departure from the urban landscape. Nestled in the tranquil part of the neighborhood, his suburban residence offered solace from the city's hustle. In contrast to the distant allure of Kennedy Towers, the suburban milieu enveloped Aaron, concealing the iconic skyline from his immediate surroundings. The gentle glow of the tower lights danced on the distant horizon, teasingly out of reach from where Aaron stood, inviting contemplation on life's intricate mysteries.

*****

In the dimly lit courtyard of Kennedy Towers, the early morning hours held a sinister secret. A lifeless body lay sprawled in the middle of the courts, a grim spectacle that had attracted the attention of a few residents huddled in separate groups, exchanging speculative whispers. The air was thick with tension as a pair of police officers and the coroner worked diligently to unravel the mystery surrounding the unknown victim.

Among the gathered law enforcement officers, Detective Aguilar, known for his sharp wit and penchant for gambling, sauntered onto the scene. His keen eyes darted to the lifeless figure, and he interrupted the ongoing chatter.

"I'll bet my next paycheck that one of these degenerates from this complex was high on something and did this. It's crazy what they do to their own people," asserted the local Police Officer. Detective Aguilar, unfazed by the comment, interjected confidently, "I'll take that bet. In fact, I'll throw in my drinking purse and alimony that it was someone from outside of this community. These guys over here don't get down like this. This guy must be what, in his late fifties? This was more like a message being sent from someone outside these walls."

Slightly offended, the Police Officer muttered, "Who's this prick think he is, butting in like he Sherlock Holmes or something?"

Detective Aguilar, maintaining his calm demeanor, replied, "Nope, no Sherlock. Just a guy who has a bit of a gambling problem that's trying to scrape up a few dollars, roughly about the same amount as your 'next paycheck.'" As tensions escalated, the other Police Officer intervened, recognizing Detective Aguilar's badge and rank and gesturing his partner to back off. The banter continued, with Detective Weber joining the scene.

"Giving the 'Boys in Blue' a hard time again?" Detective Weber quipped.

"Someone has to keep it fun around here," Aguilar responded.

The detectives engaged in a discussion about the crime, contemplating the possibilities. Detective Aguilar sought more details about the crime scene, probing for clues about the victim's identity and the circumstances surrounding the incident. Detective Weber shared critical information about a lone witness who saw two figures dressed in black fleeing the scene. The detectives surmised that the absence of loud gunshots suggested the use of a silencer, implying a meticulous plan to avoid detection.

Their conversation was abruptly interrupted by the anguished wails of an unknown woman. She approached the scene in distress, crying out, "Tommy! No! Tommy! Oh my God, please, no!" The woman's desperate cries cut through the air as she attempted to push through the detectives to reach the lifeless body. Detective Aguilar gently restrained her, preventing her from getting too close, and she eventually yielded, burying her face in the detective's jacket.

In the heart of Kennedy Towers, a dark mystery had unfolded, and the echoes of grief and uncertainty reverberated through the courtyard. Detective Aguilar and Detective Weber now faced the daunting task of untangling the web of secrets that shrouded the life and death of the unknown victim.

Chapter 7:

Bonds Renewed

Detective Weber's voice cut through the air, urging his fellow officers and the coroner to expedite the investigation. The scene, shrouded in the cold reality of a crime, contrasted starkly with the warmth that emanated from Cooley's apartment later that evening.

In the heart of Kennedy Towers, Cooley's place became a haven for laughter and camaraderie. The apartment buzzed with the lively energy of women gathered for Cooley's small birthday gathering. Cooley, adorned in a cheap Brazilian hair weave and makeup, held court in the spotlight, regaling the group with entertaining anecdotes and humorous observations.

"And that Brandi, she's a real Hussy, always in someone else's business, her old stiff, uptight, Gayle, before I met Oprah-looking ass," Cooley exclaimed, prompting laughter from the assembled women. The air filled with the shared joy of gossip, an escape from the everyday challenges they faced.

Cooley's storytelling continued, each tale more outrageous than the last. The women, including Tanashia and Kiki, found solace in the lightness of the moment, their laughter echoing through the walls of the apartment. As Cooley delved into the latest neighborhood drama, the women eagerly joined in the laughter, finding respite in the levity of the evening. The gossip flowed freely, creating a bond that transcended the struggles of their daily lives.

However, the carefree atmosphere took a turn when Cooley shifted the topic to a scandal involving an older man and a young woman. The laughter continued, albeit with an edge of discomfort, as Kiki revealed that the man in question was her friend Roxy's sugar daddy.

"Guess she just gonna have to drop that ass on them poles a little harder now," Cooley remarked, the humor tinged with an acknowledgment of the harsh realities many faced in their pursuit of financial stability. The lighthearted banter continued, but the mood shifted when Tanashia received a phone call that cut through the revelry. Her expression transformed as she absorbed the news, the carefree atmosphere dissipating into the urgency of the moment.

"I have to go. Can you give me a ride up the street?" Tanashia implored Kiki, her tone conveying the gravity of the situation.

Cooley, momentarily interrupted in her performance, voiced his displeasure. "Uh uh! Where you heffas think y'all going?" However, Tanashia's sense of duty prevailed, and she expressed her apologies before making a swift exit.

As Tanashia left, Cooley, with a wave of his hand, dismissed the departure, offering a sassy farewell. The apartment, once filled with laughter and jest, now bore the weight of real-world concerns. The revelry continued, but the undertone of life's complexities lingered—a reminder that in Kennedy Towers, moments of joy and struggles intertwined, creating a tapestry of resilience and shared experience.

*****

The cold dawn at St. Luke's Medical Center marked a turning point for Tanashia and Aaron. Emerging from the hospital, Tanashia thanked Kiki and assured her she would be in touch. The ER lobby became the stage for an emotional reunion between siblings, their family now entwined in concern for their father.

Aaron remained frozen, staring at Tanashia across the space that stretched between them like a chasm of lost years. Memories flickered in his mind: pigtails pulled, toy guns brandished, shared giggles echoing through his "Aunt" Tracy's sun-drenched kitchen. His "Nae Nae," so small and bright, was now a woman with eyes that held both the shadows of time and a surprising spark of warmth.

Squinting, "Is that you, Nae Nae?" he repeated, his voice thick with disbelief.

A smile bloomed on Tanashia's face, erasing the worry lines etched by the events of the night. "Yeah, Aaron," she said, her voice husky with emotion. "It's me."

He stumbled forward, drawn by an invisible thread woven from shared history. The awkward hug that followed was tight, a silent release of unspoken words and tangled emotions. Years rolled back in that embrace, the familiar scent of her jasmine shampoo a bridge across the distance that had grown between them.

Pulling back, Aaron scanned her face, taking in the unfamiliar contours of adulthood. "Wow," he breathed, tracing the line of her jaw with his gaze. "You've... you've changed."

She laughed, a light tinkling sound that chased away the heaviness hanging in the air. "Me? You haven't seen change until you see yourself, kiddo. You're taller, for one. And that scrawny beanpole frame has filled out nicely."

Aaron grinned, a hint of his childhood mischief sparking in his eyes. "I try my best," he teased, flexing his bicep playfully.

Their banter, light and familiar, felt like a balm on the raw wound of his father's sudden illness. It was a bridge, shaky yet strong, connecting their fractured past to the uncertain present.

Tracy met Tanashia in the ER lobby, delivering news that jolted the siblings' world. Their father, Cole, had been found unconscious, and the doctors, while optimistic about his recovery, were uncertain about the cause. As they grappled with the uncertainty, Aaron stormed into the ER, his youthful concern etched across his face.

Security restrictions in the hospital brought a momentary halt, but Tracy, seizing the role of protector, swiftly intervened. With a reassuring touch on Aaron's hand, she guided him through the bureaucracy, earning gratitude from the young man who found comfort in the chaos. Aaron's initial confusion upon seeing Tanashia gradually transformed into recognition, and the two siblings shared a warm embrace, momentarily stepping away from the weight of their father's condition.

The hospital staff ushered them into a waiting area, and a nurse shared some words of encouragement. Tanashia, Aaron, and Tracy settled into the solarium, its calm ambiance contrasting with the storm of emotions that raged within them.

As the hands of time moved relentlessly forward, conversations in the solarium painted a picture of their past, revealing glimpses of a family's fractured history and the complexities woven into the fabric of their lives.

In the midst of the somber atmosphere, Tracy, seeking a brief respite, engaged Tanashia and Aaron in memories of their childhood. The shared laughter and nostalgia offered a brief escape from the hospital's sterile walls, hinting at the bonds that once connected them.

*****

The night unfolded in snippets, traversing the realities of Kennedy Towers, where Damon and his companions found themselves entangled with Detective Aguilar and his probing questions. The tension of the encounter subsided, but not before revealing a history between Damon and the detective. In another realm of Kennedy Towers, Cooley's birthday celebration continued, momentarily eclipsing the harsh realities of life in the projects. Cooley's charisma and humor became a temporary sanctuary, providing moments of levity for those seeking refuge from the unforgiving streets.

As dawn approached, the narrative shifted back to St. Luke's Medical Center, where the siblings sat by their father's bedside. The nurse's gentle wake-up call signaled a new chapter in their collective story. Entering Cole's room, the siblings found their father in a state of semi-coherence, uttering words that pierced the air with an unexpected revelation. Lou Gehrig's disease—a haunting diagnosis that hung heavily in the room, ushering in a new chapter filled with uncertainty.

The fluorescent lights of St. Luke's solarium flickered to life, casting long, skeletal shadows across the worn furniture. Aaron and Tanashia stirred, roused from their uneasy sleep by a gentle nudge from the new morning nurse. Tracy, ever the early bird, had already flitted out of the hospital, her absence leaving a tangible void.

"Hey, guys," the nurse chirped, sunlight glinting off her starched uniform. "Your father's awake and would love to see you."

Hope flickered in their eyes, a fragile flame resisting the encroaching darkness. As they entered Cole's room, his voice, raspy but laced with wry humor, greeted them.

"Am I in heaven?" he joked, squinting at them through sleep-crusted eyes. "Because I know two angels when I see them."

A shared laugh bubbled up, a balm on the raw edges of their worry. They surrounded him, eager questions tumbling from their lips. But the joy was short-lived, replaced by a chilling truth when Cole mentioned the dreaded acronym – ALS.

Aaron, his face crumpling, bolted from the room, leaving behind the echo of his choked sob. Tanashia, her heart thundering in her chest, turned to her father, seeking answers in his faded eyes.

"It's kind of hard for me to explain, sweetheart," Cole rasped, his voice laced with a weary acceptance. "Hell, I barely understood that doctor myself. But I can tell you the honest truth: it's not looking good for me."

The words hung in the air, a death knell to their hopes. Cole, their anchor, their lighthouse in the storm, was adrift. And they, lost and terrified, clung to his every word.

"Now listen," he continued, his voice firming despite his weakness. "I need you to hear me out. My biggest regret in life was not fighting hard enough to have you two raised around one another. But now that you're old enough to make your own decisions, I want you, from this day forth, to keep each other close. I know there's a lot to catch up on, but that's your little brother. You're gonna need him as much as he needs you, now more than ever."

Tears welled in Tanashia's eyes, her voice cracking as she whispered, "Dad, please, don't say that."

Cole, his hand reaching out to cup her face, pressed on. "Listen, you two are my remaining blessings. This is life. Just please promise me you'll look out for him. I know he's younger than you, but I'm sure there are some things you can learn from him, too. Can you do that for me?"

In the hushed room, a fragile promise bloomed. "Yes, Daddy," Tanashia choked out, her voice thick with emotion.

Cole, a faint smile playing on his lips, squeezed her hand. "Thanks, baby. Go get your brother and tell him to get back in here before I come get him myself."

Tanashia, her heart heavy with the weight of his words, found Aaron in the solarium, his face pale and eyes downcast. He shared his perspective, the doctor's prognosis, the unspoken fear that hung in the air like a shroud.

"A semester ago," Aaron mumbled, his voice lost in despair, "I had to choose a baseball player for an essay. I never heard of Lou Gehrig, so I chose him. I swear I wish I didn't."

The shared pain, a raw echo of their father's illness, forged a new bond between them. Tanashia, her voice surprisingly steady, pulled him up. "Well, right now, he needs you. He needs us to be strong for him. And most importantly, he needs us to be here for each other."

A thin smile touched Aaron's lips, the echo of a promise. He pulled her close, a wordless vow binding them together in the face of their shared grief.

The following weeks blurred into a kaleidoscope of stolen moments. Aaron, his heart heavy but his spirit resolute, became Tanashia's anchor. They were at his bedside, laughing and sharing memories, refusing to let the encroaching shadow dim his light.

The subsequent conversation between father and children unfolded with a mixture of gravity and familial love. Cole, acknowledging his regrets and longing for unity, implored Tanashia and Aaron to look out for each other once he was gone.

The scene painted a poignant tableau of familial bonds, strained and strengthened by time. The promise made in that moment would become a guiding force for Tanashia and Aaron as they faced an uncertain future.

As the music of life played, scenes depicted: Aaron guiding Tanashia through an art museum, a one-on-one basketball game between the two held inside the thorough courtyard of Kennedy Towers, Kiki's growing pregnancy, shared moments at the movies, and the challenges faced by Leticia and Tracy. Amidst the tapestry of life, the thread of Cole's decline was woven into the narrative, symbolizing the inexorable march of time. Aaron and Tanashia, united by shared experiences, found solace in each other's company. In a quiet moment of prayer within an empty church, the siblings faced the inevitable challenges ahead.

*****

The baseball stadium in Rahway buzzed with excitement, but for Aaron, the game ended in frustration. As the final pitch sailed into the center fielder's glove, sealing their defeat, he slammed his bat down. Disappointment etched his face, mirroring the sentiments of his teammates. Leticia, Jacqueline, and Tino approached him, offering words of comfort and encouragement. Tanashia, seemingly out of nowhere, joined the gathering, and Aaron's introductions left his family bewildered.

Leticia struggled to conceal this thunderstrike as she confronted the reality of Aaron's rekindled connection with Tanashia. The unexpected reunion unfolded amidst the backdrop of a baseball stadium, where cheers and disappointment blended into a symphony of emotions.

The echo of the final out hung heavy in the air, a bitter symphony of cheers and dejected sighs. Aaron slammed his bat into the grass, the frustration of defeat etched on his face. Yet, amidst the sting of loss, a warmth blossomed in his chest. Tanashia stood near the dugout, her presence a beacon of comfort in the swirling fog of emotions.

Their hug, born of shared grief and newfound kinship, was a silent testament to the years they had missed. The awkward stares of his family, the raised eyebrows, and the hushed whispers only served to highlight the chasm that had separated them for so long.

"Don't worry," Tanashia murmured, pulling away from the embrace. "He's gonna be proud of you either way."

Her words, simple yet potent, were a balm to his raw spirit. He could almost see his father, his face weathered but eyes alight with pride, cheering him on from the confines of his hospital bed. The thought lifted a corner of the weight pressing down on him.

Leticia's intrusion, polite yet laced with unspoken judgment, shattered the fragile moment. The surprise on her face, the thinly veiled disapproval, spoke volumes about the secrets and tensions that had festered for years. Aaron bristled, exerting a stern protective embrace, and towered in front of Tanashia.

A bad-timed humorous introduction fell short as Caleb approached the non-verbal squabble. "Yo bro, that's her? Hook me up." Now noticing the crossfire he had just walked into, Caleb stepped away while pointing in the direction where he could be found. "Well, what's with the face, mom? You know who she is," Aaron spat, bitterness lacing his voice.

Tanashia, sensing the brewing storm, stepped forward. "I'm going to head out, Aaron," she said softly, her eyes flitting nervously to Leticia. "I'll let you know when I get in."

Leticia gave a tight smile, the effort evident. "Nice meeting you," she offered, but the words rang hollow against the backdrop of simmering resentment.

In the aftermath of the game, as the family dynamic shifted, Tanashia consoled her disappointed brother. The absence of their father, Cole, loomed heavily over the moment, casting shadows on Aaron's achievements. Tanashia's words sought to bridge the emotional gap, reassuring him that their father's pride transcended the outcome of a baseball game. "You sure you ok getting home," Aaron insisted. "Yeah, I'm good, bro," replied Tanashia.

As Tanashia hurried away, the weight of his family's fractured past settled on Aaron like a shroud. The reunion he had longed for, the unspoken promises exchanged at his father's bedside, felt threatened by the ghosts of old conflicts. Reaching the bus stop, Tanashia watched in despair as the last bus rumbled away, leaving her stranded in the waning light. Panic gnawed at her edges, the loneliness of the abandoned street amplifying her anxieties.

Frantic, she pulled out her phone, dialing Cooley only to be met with his absent voicemail. Whiz, her last hope, answered on the second ring, his voice an unwelcoming lifeline.

"Yo, get that piece of shit off the road! I swear if he would've hit my ride, I would've popped a hole in the back of his neck!" Whiz redirected to Tanashia on the phone, "Ayo, where you at?"

"I'm by the Baseball Stadium in Rahway. Can you come?" she pleaded, her voice trembling.

"Bet! I'm on my way." Whiz assured, his words tinged with concern and annoyance.

The minutes stretched into an eternity, each tick of the clock a relentless drumbeat of worry. Alone and vulnerable, Tanashia stood guard against the encroaching shadows, her heart a fragile ember defying the darkness. Coming from such dangerous grounds, there was a bit of irony in the trepidation and internal panic Tanashia felt whenever she was out of her locality.

The rumble of an engine, a beacon of salvation in the twilight, shattered the tense silence. Whiz's familiar cherry-red Impala skidded to a halt, his concerned face breaking into a relieved grin.

*****

The revelation of Tanashia's existence left Leticia and Jacqueline in a state of shock. The unspoken complexities of the family's history began to surface, threatening the fragile balance between acceptance and confusion.

The car rolled to a stop in front of their house, the engine sputtering its final sigh. The tension inside mirrored the heavy silence outside, an oppressive fog that choked off communication.

Stepping out into the cool night air, Aaron slammed the car door shut, the clang echoing like a declaration of war. Leticia followed her face, a mask of hurt and anger. They stood across from each other, two soldiers preparing for battle on the familiar battlefield of their fractured family.

"I know that you think you're doing what's right," Leticia finally said, her voice tight with controlled emotion. "But I don't think you should be wasting your time with her. You have other things to worry about, like school and your future."

Aaron bristled, his jaw clenching with defiance. "And dad? What about him? Look, I don't need your approval. She's my sister, and she has been the best thing that has happened to me since I can remember, so yes, I do have things to think about, especially my future, which will include her in it, whether you like it or not!"

His words, fueled by frustration and growing resentment, hung in the air like a sour taste. Leticia flinched, a flicker of pain momentarily breaking through her carefully constructed facade.

Leticia rumbled. Her voice was jarringly loud in the quiet suburban neighborhood. "Aaron, don't you dare talk to me that way. I'm your mother! I raised you damn near alone. Don't you forget that!"

Aaron hastily responded, "And I'm sure it's your fault that you were all alone!"

Leticia ejected a vigorous slap across Aaron's face. Stumbling back, a comforting hand suppresses his stinging cheek. The anger in his eyes bled into hurt, the years of unspoken conflict bubbling over.

"So now what? You gonna kick me out, too?" he retorted, his voice thick with bitterness.

Leticia's shoulders slumped, the fight momentarily drained from her face. "Oh, is that what he told you?" she asked, her voice laced with a deep-seated pain.

Aaron, caught off guard by the unexpected question, faltered. "No, he didn't have to," he muttered, looking away. "I paid attention over the years, and I see how things are and how they'll always be, 'your way or no way at all.' But from here on out, things will not play out that way, and if I got to stay at Caleb's house, I will."

The threat hung heavy in the air, a stark reminder of the chasm that had grown between them over the years. Leticia, her eyes filled with a deep, unspoken sorrow, simply shook her head.

"Nope, not necessary," she said, her voice weary. "Do as you wish. I just hope one day I don't have to be the one to say, 'I told you so.'"

With those words, she turned and walked towards the house, her retreating figure a lonely silhouette against the dimly lit porch light. Aaron, left alone in the driveway, stared after her, his heart heavy with a conflicting mix of anger, resentment, and a gnawing feeling of guilt.

As the silence stretched between them, he realized that the battle with his mother was just the tip of the iceberg. The real struggle, the one that threatened to consume him, was the one raging within himself. The pain of his father's illness, the uncertainty of his future, and the weight of his fractured family were burdens he no longer knew how to navigate.

Standing there, bathed in the cold moonlight, Aaron looked up at the vast expanse of the night sky. A single star, bright and defiant, winked back at him. At that moment, he made a silent vow. He would fight for himself, for Tanashia, for his father, and for the family he so desperately wanted to believe in.

But how did one fight against the ghosts of the past, the unspoken resentments, and the fear of a future that seemed increasingly uncertain? He didn't have the answers, but he knew he couldn't let the darkness win. He had to find the light, the spark of hope that would lead him through the maze of his complicated life.

The journey ahead would be fraught with challenges and heartbreak, but one thing was sure: Aaron would walk it, not alone, but with the newfound strength of a family, albeit a fractured one, and the flicker of a love that promised a brighter dawn.

The night air, no longer oppressive, felt charged with a sense of resolve. He took a deep breath, the chill biting into his lungs, and turned towards the house. He didn't know what awaited him inside, but he knew one thing for sure: the battle was far from over.

******

Caleb's uncensored comment added an awkward layer to the situation, accentuating the discomfort that lingered between the family members. As Tanashia made her departure, a sense of tension clung to the air. Outside the stadium, Tanashia's plans were disrupted by the absence of the last bus.

The night air rushed through the open windows of Whiz's speeding car, carrying with it the beats of the blasting music. Tanashia, tense and uneasy, spoke up.

"Could you slow down?" she pleaded.

"Chill out, I got this," Whiz responded confidently.

"Damn, I didn't call you to have us locked up or killed!"

Tanashia's eyes caught sight of a medicine bottle in the cup holder, and she reached for it.

"Whiz, what are these?" she inquired.

Whiz swatted her hand away, snapping, "Don't touch my shit!"

"Don't hit my hand like I'm some damn child!" Tanashia retorted.

"Do I put my hands on your shit?" Whiz countered, snatching Tanashia's phone away. "Huh?" He examined the phone. "Who the hell is 'Baby Boy'? This who you was with? So this why I ain't heard from ya hoe ass?"

"That's my brother, dumbass! Hoe? I am not your ex, who was in a whole 'nother relationship with your best friend."

"Don't give me that 'brother' shit. You only got one brother; punk ass Damon."

"Whatever, Whiz, just give me back my phone, please."

The car pulled up outside Kennedy Towers, but Whiz wasn't ready to let the argument end.

"Nah, we ain't done yet. You gonna tell me who this other nigga is, or on God, I'll break this shit!"

Tanashia retaliated by snatching the pills. "Yeah, and I swear I'll throw this shit right over that gate."

A struggle ensued in the car as they tussled over the pills. A concerned bystander, a local guy, took notice.

"Nae, you good?" he asked.

Whiz, still agitated, brandished his gun. "Yeah, nigga, she good! You good?"

The bystander replied, "Yeah, fam, we good, you got that." Tanashia managed to break free and exit the car. The local guy hustled into the towers to inform Damon about the confrontation.

"Yo, Dame, that punk ass fool Whiz out there wildin'. He got your sister ragged up in the car. He whipped out on me when I went to go check him."

"What?" Damon furiously exclaimed. Concerned, Snatch immediately took charge. "Yo, go strap up," Snatch militantly obliges, drilling a few of their goons. "Yeah, do that, but y'all stay back. I don't want this scary ass fool to start busting out of fear. I got this," replies Damon.

"Nah, bro, I'm coming with you," Snatch insisted.

Damon reassured the safety of everyone, "A'ight, bet. Just don't make any sudden moves. Don't want this scary nigga doing anything stupid. Matter of fact, give Shorty your piece."

Snatch, uncertain about the decision, replied, "Word? You sure about this, bro? A'ight man, whatever." Snatch reluctantly handed the gun to his friend. "Let's go handle this fool."

As Whiz caught up with Tanashia, tensions escalated. He cornered her against a car, demanding the return of his belongings.

"Yo, I'm not gonna keep asking you to give me my shit! I'm done with your selfish ass anyway. Only call when you're stranded or need something."

"I don't need shit from you, just give me my phone, and leave me the fuck alone."

Unbeknownst, Damon had snuck up behind Whiz and began choking him.

"I told you if you ever put your hands on my sister again, I was gonna kill you, didn't I!" Damon asserted.

Gasping for air, Whiz felt Damon release his grip and push him to the ground. His gun fell out, and Snatch picked it up.

"Yo, we good. I ain't tryna beef with you," Whiz gasped, face down and back turned away. "Just give me my perks and my nine, and I'll be on my way. I don't want no problems." He threw Tanashia's phone toward her. "Take your phone, so you can call up your other nigga when you stranded."

Using the phone toss as a diversion, Whiz sought an opportunity to attack as he reached for a knife in his pocket, plotting his next move.

*****

The aftermath of the chaotic events at Kennedy Towers left the air heavy with tension. Damon, with Snatch in tow, parted ways with Tanashia and Kiki, both parties grappling with the consequences of a violent altercation. In the car, Damon's stern instructions echoed as they wrestled with the unfolding reality. At Kiki's house, a somber atmosphere took hold. Tanashia, still reeling from the clash with Whiz and the abrupt departure of Damon, grappled with the weight of recent events. Kiki's attempts to soothe her fell short, and the realization of the fractured ties within her family seemed insurmountable.

Meanwhile, the drama unfolded in Aaron's household. Leticia's attempt to dissuade him from pursuing a connection with Tanashia escalated into a heated argument. The emotional rift between mother and son widened, exposing the underlying issues that had long festered beneath the surface.

As tensions mounted, the narrative shifted to the tumultuous scene outside Kennedy Towers. Damon's decision to confront Whiz had unforeseen consequences, leaving Tanashia grappling with the aftermath of the violent encounter. The sudden urgency to reach the hospital and Damon's poignant farewell left Tanashia emotionally raw.

Whiz's menacing charge toward Damon was abruptly halted as Snatch, in a panic, fired a shot into Whiz's stomach. Damon, shocked, realized the severity of the situation.

"Oh shit! Yo, let's get the fuck out of here!" Damon urged, pulling Tanashia away.

"We can't leave him like this!" Tanashia cried, her heart torn between loyalty and fear.

"Let's go, Nae! This shit's on him!" Damon insisted, guiding Tanashia away from the chaotic scene.

As they sought refuge at Kiki's house, the reality of their actions weighed heavily on them.

"Yo! What the hell? How the hell are we gonna get out of this?" Damon questioned, his mind racing.

Kiki, attempting to comfort Tanashia, offered her a cup of water. "Baby, try to relax. Here, drink."

Shaking and crying, Tanashia lamented, "We just left him."

Panicking, Snatch voiced his regret. "I messed up! OG! I messed up big time, bruh!"

Damon, trying to console Snatch, asserted, "Listen, brother; you did what you had to do. If it wasn't for you, I probably wouldn't be here, feel me? Beloved, you ain't got shit to worry about. As far as I'm concerned, you were never there."

"Nah, G, I can't go out like that," Snatch protested.

"Listen, that's how it's gonna be, no other way," Damon declared, extending his hand for a promissory shake.

In a moment of understanding, Snatch shook Damon's hand. "Love you, my guy. Your family is my family, no matter what."

"Love you, bro," Damon reciprocated.

"Hit my jack if anything. I'm a lay low at one of my new shorty's cribs. Stay up, big homie," announced Snatch, heading to the door. "Can she be trusted?" Damon asked in concern. "OG, the boys can come knocking while I'm 'in it,' and she would say she doesn't know me. Feel me, bro?" Snatch confidently retorted. Snatch daps Damon then leaves Kiki's apartment.

Tanashia, still shaken, received multiple calls from her concerned mother. Swiftly, Damon advises her not to answer until they have figured things out.

"Did anyone see y'all?" Kiki inquired.

"A few of my homies know what went down, but they are good. Other than that, I don't know, love. Shit happened so fast," Damon explained.

Amidst the chaos, Tanashia checked her voicemail, and her reaction was immediate.

"I have to go! I have to go now!" she exclaimed, her urgency apparent.

"You can't go see him, I can't let you..." Damon demanded.

Tanashia interjected, "It's my father! He went into cardiac arrest!" Tanashia pleaded, "I need to see him!"

Realizing the gravity of the situation, Damon instructed Kiki to take Tanashia to the hospital, cautioning Tanashia about interacting with the police.

"Ok, Kiki, take her to the hospital. Nae, if you run into any police, don't say anything other than you two were together earlier, and he dropped you off. Nothing about me or my whereabouts, you got that?" Damon warned.

Tanashia nodded her head in agreement, and as she left, Damon took a moment to express his regret and support to her.

"Listen, I'm sorry for what you had to see earlier, and even sorrier for what you're going through with your pops. Just stay strong, a'ight, baby girl?" Damon offered words of comfort, giving her a soft head butt before she departed.

At the hospital, emotions ran high as Kiki, Tracy, and Aaron met Tanashia outside Cole's room. The news of Cole's passing hit them hard.

"You two meant so much to him," Tracy said, consoling them. "I tell ya, it's all he ever talked about. I'm sure him seeing you two together was very comforting during his last moments."

Tanashia, still in disbelief, questioned, "How'd it just happen so fast?"

"I know. We were just hanging out after one of my games. He was dealing with so much pain," Aaron shared. "I don't know how he handled it the way he did."

As they gathered outside Cole's room, a chaplain approached, offering words of comfort and leading them in a moment of prayer. The four stood over Cole's lifeless body, finding solace in the scripture recitation, seeking strength to face the challenges ahead.

The hospital became the stage for another heart-wrenching episode. Cole's sudden cardiac arrest sent shockwaves through the family. Aaron, Tracy, and Tanashia, now united by grief, faced the Chaplain for a moment of prayer. The verses from Psalms provided a bittersweet comfort, their voices rising in unison amidst the pain.

Tracy and Tanashia returned to Kennedy Towers. The attempt to resume a semblance of normalcy was disrupted by the arrival of Detective Aguilar and unmarked vehicles. As the unraveling threads of the story continued to weave through the characters' lives, the emotional toll of recent events set the stage for the next chapter in this complex, interconnected saga.

*****

Tanashia sat in the stark interrogation room, Detective Weber's harsh words echoing in her ears. The iconic good cop, bad cop strategy walloped Tanashia's mental state. The grief over her father's sudden demise and the unsettling encounter with Whiz was compounded by the looming threat of questioning by law enforcement. The atmosphere in the room was tense, an unwelcome continuation of the tumult that had engulfed her life.

Detective Weber's interrogation style was aggressive, his demeanor unyielding. Tanashia, in her vulnerable state, felt the weight of his accusations. Memories of her childhood surfaced, a stark contrast to the chaos surrounding her now.

*****

In a poignant flashback, eight-year-old Tanashia found herself in the principal's office, struggling with emotions tied to her "deceased" brother Aaron. Time and distance away from her brother created nightmares, which eventually consumed her thoughts and confused her reality. Her teacher's concern led to a misunderstanding, and her father, Cole, reassured her with a promise of ice cream and a shared secret. The innocence of that moment sharply contrasted with the harsh reality of Detective Weber's accusations.

As the interrogation intensified, Tanashia found herself grappling with the trauma of her past, her father's recent death, and the mounting pressure from law enforcement. Detective Weber's insinuations about Whiz and the bullet's connection to a previous incident heightened the stakes, leaving Tanashia in a state of distress.

Meanwhile, Tracy, her mother, waited outside, unaware of the events unfolding within the precinct walls. Shannon, Tanashia's young sister, expressed concern over a disturbing dream, inadvertently reflecting the turmoil surrounding their lives. The strained relationships within the family were exposed, leaving Tracy frustrated and perplexed by the mounting chaos.

Leticia informed Aaron about an upcoming trip. The tension in their relationship, compounded by grief and unresolved issues, manifested in a plea from Leticia for Aaron to accompany her. The delicate balance between family responsibilities and personal aspirations added another layer of complexity to the unfolding story. The threads connecting their lives tightened, and the uncertain future loomed ahead, promising more revelations and challenges for each member of this intricate tapestry.

Chapter 8:

Resolution

Tanashia navigated the intricate web of her troubled life, seeking solace in the company of Cooley, her closest confidante. The revelations about Whiz's involvement in a recent shooting and the connection to a prior murder weighed heavily on her. Damon's erratic behavior under the influence only added to the turmoil she faced.

Tracy sat in the living room, smoking a cigarette while engaging in a tense conversation with a friend on the phone.

"Girl, I don't know what the hell is going on. And I have been calling Damon and Kiki; they still haven't gotten back to me. This shit's crazy, got me stressed the hell out. Hold up, girl, she's pulling up right now. I'll call you back." Tracy hung up as Tanashia entered the apartment.

"Girl, you ready to tell me what in God's name is going on because between you and Damon..." Tracy began, her voice filled with concern.

"Mom, please, not right now," Tanashia pleaded.

"So, when the hell exactly? You get picked up by the police, tell them not to discuss anything with me, and now you are saying, 'not right now,'" Tracy questioned, her frustration evident.

Shannon, Tanashia's younger sibling, overheard the conversation and joined in.

"Nae? Where were you last night? I came to your room because I couldn't sleep, and you weren't there. Did you stay by Cooley's?" Shannon asked.

Tanashia sought an opportunity to use Shannon as a shield from Tracy's assertive questionnaire. "Babygirl."

Tracy, eyes stretched, still determined to get answers, whispered to Tanashia, "We ain't done."

Ignoring Tracy's persistence, Tanashia turned her attention to Shannon, trying to lighten the mood.

"Hey, pouty pie, what happened? You were dreaming about zombie dolphins again?" Tanashia asked playfully.

Shannon shook her head. "No. I had a dream about you, and you were screaming and crying, and there was some kind of ugly monster face covered in blood surrounding you."

Tanashia, offering reassurance, said, "And now look. Here I am. No blood, no monster faces. Just a bad dream, baby.

And as for you, no more scary movies or sweets before bed. I have to go."

Tracy interjected, "Where are you going?"

"To Cooley's for a little," Tanashia replied, rushing to the door. "Just to grab some things I left from the other night. Mom, I'll call you."

"Nae!" Tracy called after her, but the door slammed shut.

"Ugh!" Tracy sighed in frustration, left alone with her thoughts and a cigarette burning in her hand.

As Tanashia traveled to Cooley's apartment, she couldn't shake the gnawing worry for Whiz, but most importantly, Damon. The promise he extracted from her—silence at the cost of her life—echoed in her mind. The weight of secrets and the complexities of her relationships cast a shadow over her journey to check on her troubled brother.

The heavy atmosphere in Aaron's home mirrored the weight on his shoulders. Leticia, his mother, approached him with a plea amid the tumult of their lives.

"Sweetheart, I know this is a tough time for you. It is for both of us, but I really need to take this trip. You know this is the first regional event since my promotion, and I really want you to come with me. We'll be back in time for your father's funeral," Leticia explained, her tone carrying a mixture of concern and urgency.

*****

Aaron, sitting on the couch, looked at his mother with a sense of understanding. "Mom, it's fine, just go. I'll be fine."

Leticia reached out and gently touched Aaron's hand. "Listen, as bleak as it may seem, let me assure you that this is for our future, and your father would want this."

"Yeah, I'm sure you know what he'd want," Aaron replied with a hint of bitterness, unable to mask his pain.

Leticia sighed deeply, grappling with the problematic situation. "I'll tell Jacqueline to stop by and check in with you."

Aaron, his eyes expressing a mix of sadness and frustration, responded, "Mom, please don't give her a key this time. That won't be necessary."

"Ok, I won't. Well, I have a hair appointment. You still have about six hours until the flight leaves. I hope you change your mind. Later," Leticia concluded, remaining optimistic towards Aaron's decision.

Aaron, plastered in mixed emotions, turns on his video game to quiet the noise thundering in his head. "Another update, ugh," Aaron grumbled. He quietly doses off while the game begins to update.

Back from the hair salon, Leticia enters their home. As Leticia prepared to leave, a sense of urgency lingered in the air. She moved about the living room, checking off mental lists.

"Let's see; money, food, your keys, I'm sure you have. Sorry I have to rush out, but my hairdresser kept me longer than usual. Is there anything else before I go?" Leticia asked, her tone a mix of efficiency and concern.

Aaron, sitting on the couch, shook his head. "Nope."

"You sure you don't wanna come? I'll help you pack. I can spare another ten minutes or so," Leticia offered, her eyes searching for any sign of conversion in her tactics.

"No, Mom, go ahead. I'll be fine," Aaron assured.

Leticia leaned in, kissing Aaron's cheek. "Ok, sweetie."

As she pulled away, a smile on her face, Aaron expressed his love and concern. "Love you, be safe."

Leticia smiled back, reassured by the connection with her son. "Yes, sweetheart, I will. Love you."

With a final glance at Aaron, Leticia exited the apartment, leaving behind a subdued atmosphere. Aaron, left to his own devices, contemplated the challenges that lay ahead and the solitude that would accompany his mother's absence. The door closed quietly, and the apartment settled into a stillness broken only by the distant sounds of the city outside.

Left alone, Aaron sank further into the couch, contemplating the whirlwind of emotions surrounding him. The impending trip and the absence of his father created a void that seemed insurmountable. As the door closed behind Leticia, the quietness of the apartment settled in, leaving Aaron to grapple with his thoughts and the reality of the challenges ahead.

Chapter 9:

Moving Forward

Cooley's apartment provided a temporary sanctuary for Tanashia, a haven amidst the chaos that had engulfed her life. The air was thick with the scent of shared secrets and unspoken fears as Cooley, a close friend, embraced Tanashia, offering condolences for the tumultuous events.

"O.M.G. Girl, are you screwing with me right now? Because this is like some next next-level shit, and my hormones can't handle all this right now. First off, baby girl, let me give you my 'condolessons' and all," Cooley expressed with a mixture of sympathy and unintelligence, pulling Tanashia into a tight hug. "Second, Snatch did what to Whiz? You know I'm not a fan of his, but damn, I didn't expect to hear any news about that fool getting shot up."

Tanashia sighed, the weight of recent events evident in her eyes. "Well, me neither, but this was his fault. Matter of fact, it was his gun. And to make things worse, it's the same gun that was used to kill what's her-face, sugar daddy."

"Roxy?" Cooley inquired.

"Yeah, her."

"How you know?"

"That's what the detectives said while they interrogated me all last night."

"Get outta here! I hope you ain't tell them dumb-ass detectives nothing."

"No," Tanashia reassured.

"Ok. Good, you should be good then."

Just as the tension in the room seemed to ease, Tanashia's phone rang, interrupting the moment.

"Oh shit, it's Damon," Tanashia said, answering the phone. "Hello?"

Damon's voice, slurred and uneasy, came through the line. "Yo, where are you?"

"Cooley's."

"Did you hear anything about Whiz?"

"All I know is he's still alive. And his gun has a body on it, the old guy that died around here a couple of days ago."

Damon's concern deepened. "How do you know that?"

"The police took me in for questioning last night."

"Are you serious? Tell me you didn't say anything about me or Snatch being there."

"No, of course not."

"You sure? Because I know that's your nigga and all, but that motherfucker had it coming."

"I said I ain't say nothing. Could we not talk about it?"

Damon's slurred voice persisted. "Why are you mad at me? He wouldn't be laid up in a hospital if he kept his hands off you; don't forget that." Damon begins ranting. "Punk ass can't fight, so he wanna pull out knives on a motherfucker. Now look at him. And you better not say shit to nobody about this. Not to mom, not Kiki, and not to that punk ass Cooley. Not even to your fake-ass brother that you be…"

Tanashia couldn't bear the weight of his words any longer, so she hung up the phone, tears streaming down her face. Cooley stepped in, offering comfort.

"I feel so bad. It's not even late, and he's already drunk, probably high too, and when he's like that, he does dumb shit. I hate it when he drinks," Tanashia confessed.

"Where is he?" Cooley inquired.

"I don't know."

"Just call him back."

In an attempt to contact Damon, Tanashia spoke into the phone. "Hello, hello? After one ring, the phone reaches his voicemail. He's not answering. I didn't expect him to."

Cooley tried to reassure her. "He's gonna be alright. He probably gonna sleep that shit off, wake up with an ill hangover, forget the whole damn thing, and go pounce on Ms. Booty. Oooh and his girl is pregnant. You 'bout to be an auntie."

A small smile crept onto Tanashia's face amidst the turmoil. "Thanks for always being there for me."

"Come on now, what are "sisters" for?"

"Oh yeah, and one thing, Damon said if I said anything to you, he'll kill me, which means he'll kill you, too."

Cooley responded with a theatrical gesture. "About what? A bitch just caught amnesia, and I'm all out of meds."

Tanashia couldn't help but smile, grateful for the support of a true friend in these trying times.

Cooley, the vibrant and humorous friend, offered Tanashia a reprieve, a moment of laughter amid the chaos. Cooley's light-hearted banter contrasted with the dark undertones of Tanashia's reality. The seamless bond they shared provided a brief respite from the storm that brewed in the backdrop of Kennedy Towers.

"I'm a head out in a few," Tanashia announced, preparing to leave.

"Damn heffa, where you going? Your man laid up, you ain't got no job, and already went and found you a new nigga?" Cooley teased.

"No, girl. I'm going to meet up with little bro and make sure he ok," Tanashia explained.

"Awe, that's nice of you. Look at you being a big sister. I know he probably is cute as hell. Don't be holding out, sis. Ain't he half-Spanish? I know he probably got muscles and taco meat on his chesticles. Is he too young for me?" Cooley playfully inquired.

"Bye, Cooley!" Tanashia responded, brushing off the teasing.

As Tanashia headed out, Cooley continued his banter with the Uber driver, adding a touch of humor to the tense situation. Meanwhile, a mysterious person pursued in a trailing vehicle.

*****

In Aaron's apartment, Leticia ensured that her son had all he needed before her departure. The mundane checklist—a reminder of daily routines—carried an unspoken weight, a poignant acknowledgment of the fractured family dynamics. The brief exchange between mother and son hinted at a history of pain, regret, and the unspoken words that lingered between them. Back at Cooley's apartment, Tanashia faced the reality of her responsibility as a sister. Damon's ominous warning lingered, a testament to the dysfunctional relationships woven into the fabric of their lives. The line between loyalty and self-preservation blurred, leaving Tanashia grappling with the morality of her silence.

At Aaron's home, Tanashia rang the doorbell, and Aaron greeted her warmly.

"Wassup, sis? Come in," Aaron welcomed.

"Woah, Kid, this is how you living? It's beautiful out here," Tanashia observed.

What had been a moment of emptiness for Aaron now turned into a spirited decor for his lonely heart. Tanashia and Aaron marveled at the collection of items in Aaron's room, sharing laughter and memories. However, the tranquility was shattered when a mysterious person followed Tanashia to Aaron's home.

As Tanashia explored the house, Aaron proudly showcased his belongings, including a fire-proof safe with intriguing contents.

"Real fire-proof safe. Turn around so I can enter the combination," Aaron instructed.

"Fine, whatever, hurry up," Tanashia playfully responded.

Aaron revealed a collection of items, including a sharp World War II M1 Bayonet that was once attached to a soldier's rifle, along with various currencies from around the world. "Wow, you had it good, huh, silver spoon?" Tanashia implied. "You done traveled all around the world, and I barely ever left my neighborhood." Discounting his abundant upbringing, Aaron replied, "I didn't ask for any of this. In fact, I would have traded it all to have you around more." As the siblings continued to share stories, their moment was immobilized by an emergent sound of shattered glass upstairs. The atmosphere in Aaron's home shifted from a lively exploration to an unexpected nightmare.

"You heard that?" Aaron asked Tanashia.

"Yeah, what was it?" Tanashia replied.

"Jacqueline, is that you?" Aaron questioned while approaching.

The tension escalated as Aaron approached the front door, discovering a break-in attempt. Suddenly, a mysterious man emerged, and a single shot blared towards the two.

"Aaron!" Tanashia screamed as her brother dropped to the floor, a bullet piercing his chest. The mysterious man revealed himself: Damon, Tanashia's brother.

"Damon! What the hell are you doing?" Tanashia demanded.

"I don't know, I got shooked, I just reacted!" Damon explained in panic.

"You didn't have to shoot him! I'm calling the police!" Tanashia insisted.

"Nae, don't call the police!" Damon pleaded.

"Why are you here?" Tanashia questioned.

"I thought you were meeting up with Whiz. He snuck away from the hospital earlier. I figured he'd call you first and try to use you to get to me," Damon explained.

Torn between family loyalty and the chaos unfolding, Tanashia decided to call for help. She knelt beside Aaron, who was still alive but struggling for dear life.

"He's been shot! I'm calling for help!" Tanashia declared.

As she dialed emergency services, Aaron gasped for air. Damon, realizing Aaron was still alive, stood over him with his gun. The situation grew more dire as Tanashia witnessed her brother's desperation.

"He's not going to need one. He saw my face. I gotta finish this. I'm sorry, sis," Damon declared.

Damon raised his gun to deliver a fatal shot, but Tanashia jumped in front of Aaron. Desperate to prevent further tragedy, she grabbed the Bayonet that Aaron dropped and stabbed Damon in the stomach.

"Nae, what the fuh..., what did you do?" Damon exclaimed, blood staining his clothes.

As Tanashia rushed to call for help, the scene descended into chaos. The dispatcher's voice became a distant echo as Tanashia, Aaron, and Damon grappled with the consequences of their choices.

"Keep breathing, you're doing good," Tanashia reassured Aaron, her heart heavy with the weight of the unfolding tragedy.

The room filled with the sound of sirens in the distance, a dissonant melody to the chaos that had taken over Aaron's home. Tanashia, overwhelmed by the unfolding nightmare, cried out to a higher power for help.

"God! Please, help me!"

*****

The dimly lit room bore witness to the aftermath of an unimaginable tragedy. Tanashia, caught in the crossfire of her brother's misguided actions, stood paralyzed between the wounded bodies of her brothers. The gunshot's reverberations still lingered in the air, echoing the shattered fragments of what were once amicable siblings.

As Aaron lay on the floor gasping for breath, the red stain on his chest was stark a testament to the brutality that had unfolded in his supposed sanctuary. Tanashia, torn between the urgency of aiding Aaron and the overwhelming shock of Damon's betrayal, hovered in a surreal limbo, her world unraveling before her eyes. Damon, now bleeding from the stomach, writhed in pain against the wall. Tanashia's desperate attempt to prevent further bloodshed had left a cruel tableau of sibling conflict. The room, once a sanctuary, now bore the stains of an irreversible tragedy.

As Tanashia dialed 911, the weight of her choices pressed down on her. The dispatcher's voice became a distant murmur, drowned out by the whirlwind of chaos that enveloped her. The blaring sirens approaching 212 Rose Lane promised help, but the scars left by the events of that night would be indelible. The room, now marked by blood and violence, was a stark contrast to the idyllic setting of Aaron's supposed haven. The shattered glass, the metallic tang of blood, and the palpable tension in the air painted a grim picture of familial bonds torn asunder.

Tanashia knelt by Aaron's side, urging him to hold on, her voice a fragile melody against the cacophony of sirens and her own anguished sobs. The scene unfolded like a tragic play, with each character playing a role in a narrative of pain and betrayal. Damon's lifeless body served as a chilling reminder of the consequences that stemmed from a spiral of violence and desperation. The big bro-little sis bond that had once held them together now lay shattered, fragments of trust scattered on the floor. As the EMTs rushed into the room, the harsh glare of the ambulance lights illuminated the stark reality of the situation.

Tanashia, still reeling from the shock, was guided out of the room as the paramedics began their urgent work. The flashing lights cast an otherworldly glow on the scene as if the universe itself bore witness to the tragedy that unfolded at 212 Rose Lane.

In the hushed moments that followed, Tanashia stood outside, her eyes fixed on the chaotic tableau within. The night air felt heavy with unspoken grief, a silent witness to the fractured bonds that lay in ruins. The room, once a sanctuary, now stood as a chilling testament to the irreversible consequences of choices made in desperation. The shattered echoes of that fateful night would resonate in Tanashia's life, leaving scars that transcended the physical realm.

Chapter 10:

Epilogue

The cemetery, shrouded in quiet stillness, became a sacred space for the grieving souls who had gathered to bid farewell to Cole Anderson. The air hung heavy with grief, thick with the unspoken pain that accompanied the departure of a loved one. Mourners, their faces etched with sorrow, clustered around the freshly dug grave.

Leticia, dressed in somber black, stood alongside the crowd, her eyes fixed on Tanashia, who seemed lost in her own world of grief. Tracy, a pillar of silent strength, stood by Tanashia's side, offering comfort through a simple yet profound presence. The atmosphere was charged with raw emotion as the pastor's words, a distant murmur, blended seamlessly with the soft sobs that echoed through the somber air.

The pastor's voice, a soothing balm for wounded hearts, carried the weight of solemnity as he began to eulogize Cole. His words, carefully chosen and delivered with a comforting cadence, resonated across the gathering, bringing a measure of solace to the mourners.

"Hold thou thy cross before my closing eyes, shine through the gloom, and point me to the skies: Heaven's morning breaks and the earth's vain shadows flee; in life, in death, O Lord, abide with me," intoned the pastor, his voice rising and falling with the rhythm of shared grief.

The collective response of "Amen" rippled through the assembly, a united plea for divine comfort in the face of profound loss. It was a moment of communal prayer, where the shared sorrow of the gathered souls formed an unspoken bond that transcended the boundaries of individual grief.

As the pastor continued to paint a vivid picture of Cole's life, his accomplishments, and the cherished memories he left behind, Leticia's thoughts turned to Aaron. In the midst of the poignant ceremony, she bent down to kiss him gently on the forehead. Aaron, seated quietly in his wheelchair, observed the rituals with a solemnity that belied his young age.

The cemetery, with its neatly arranged rows of headstones and the gnarled branches of ancient trees, became a sanctuary for those grappling with the ephemeral nature of life. Each gravestone told a unique story, a testament to the diverse paths that converged and diverged within the tapestry of human existence.

Tanashia, lost in the labyrinth of grief, clutched a small bouquet of lilies, Cole's favorite flowers. Tracy, sensing Tanashia's need for solace, offered a silent hand of support.

Unexpectedly, a second hand gently locks onto Tanashia's. It was Leticia's. Tanashia kindly embraced the comfort. Together, they navigated the emotional landscape of farewell, where words were often inadequate, and shared presence spoke volumes.

The eulogy painted a portrait of Cole as a man of integrity, kindness, and love. Friends and family nodded in agreement as the pastor recounted stories that illuminated the essence of the departed soul. The resonance of shared memories provided a semblance of connection, a bridge between the tangible world and the ethereal realm where Cole's spirit now dwelled.

As the pastor concluded his eulogy, the cemetery seemed to hold its breath in collective reverence. The finality of the moment hung in the air, and the reality of Cole's absence settled into the hearts of those who had known and loved him.

The mourners, guided by an unspoken understanding, began to disperse, each grappling with their grief in their own way. Some lingered by the gravesite, seeking a quiet moment of reflection, while others sought solace in the company of loved ones. The cemetery, a silent witness to countless farewells, embraced the ebb and flow of human emotions with stoic grace.

Leticia, Tanashia, and Tracy formed a small cluster, finding comfort in the shared silence that bound them together. The cemetery, with its hallowed ground, became a sanctuary for the living to navigate the complex emotions that accompany the departure of a cherished soul.

The sun dipped below the horizon, casting long shadows over the gravestones. The sky, painted in hues of orange and purple, seemed to echo the emotions of the mourners. As the day surrendered to night, the cemetery transformed into a realm where memories and echoes of the past lingered like guardian spirits.

In the quiet aftermath of the ceremony, Leticia guided Aaron's wheelchair towards the exit, a motherly hand resting on his shoulder. The journey through the cemetery became a metaphor for the broader journey of life — a path marked by farewells but also illuminated by the enduring light of shared love and memories.

Though forgiving, Leticia's motherly instincts were prioritized. "Say bye to her, Aaron," said Leticia as she transported him to the car. Aaron rescinded, resting his hands on both sides of the wheelchair to brake.

"I know you feel like it's her fault, Mom, but it's not. She's my sister," Aaron affirmed, his determination evident.

In response, Leticia, emotions tinged with frustration, throws her hands to the sky and retorts, "Aaron! Es tu vida. Haz lo que quieres!"

In response to Aaron's indecision, Leticia discontinued her reprimand. Though silent, her emotions simmering beneath the surface, tinged with frustration. Although her words were few, the weight of her silence spoke volumes. With a weary exhale, she chose not to engage further, knowing that any attempt to sway Aaron's decision would likely fall on deaf ears. As Aaron deliberated over his choices, Leticia's silence became a declaration—a silent protest against the cycle of indecision that seemed to perpetually orbit their relationship. With each passing moment, she felt herself growing weary of the emotional rollercoaster, longing for a sense of stability and clarity that seemed perpetually out of reach.

In the quiet depths of her soul, Leticia made a silent vow to herself—to no longer invest her energy in trying to steer Aaron towards a path of certainty. She was done with the endless dance of uncertainty, ready to embrace whatever course Aaron chose, even if it meant drifting further apart.

She walked away, leaving Aaron resolute in his decision. Maneuvering his wheelchair through the sea of mourners, he moved toward Tanashia, determined to bridge the growing gap within the family.

The cemetery, a tableau of sorrow and parting words, framed the unfolding drama of a fractured family in the wake of loss.

Aaron struggled to wheel himself over to Tanashia, who quickly ran to his side.

"What you trying to do, bust out your stitches? You ok?" Tanashia asked, concern etched across her face.

"Yeah, I'm good. Doc said I'll start therapy next week and should be back to normal in about a month or so," Aaron replied, managing a weak smile.

"That's good, right?" Tanashia said, her eyes searching his for reassurance.

"Yeah. How about you? I'm sorry about how everything happened. I'm here for you if you need me. I'll even come to the funeral with you to help you get through it," Aaron offered genuine concern in his voice.

"Listen. You don't have anything to be sorry about. And, no, I'll be fine. You just focus on getting better," Tanashia insisted, guiding the wheelchair towards the family car.

Detective Aguilar approached the two of them, and Tracy, Tanashia's mother, intervened.

"Officer? Is everything ok?" Tracy asked, concern furrowing her brows.

"Yes, Ma'am, everything's just fine. I'm just going to have a word with these two," Detective Aguilar replied, glancing at Tanashia and Aaron. Tracy, realizing she wasn't included to be a part of the conversation, slightly steps aside.

"Oh ok, well, I'll be right over there if you need anything. And please, sir, no surprise takeaways today?" Tracy chuckled weakly, attempting to lighten the heavy atmosphere.

"Thank you, Ma'am. I'll try not to," Detective Aguilar said, acknowledging Tracy before turning his attention back to Tanashia and Aaron.

"First and foremost, I want to again say that I'm terribly sorry about your father. I've known him over the years; he always was a straightforward guy. And Tanashia, I'm sorry about your brother. We had our ups and downs, but overall, he wasn't that bad of a guy. Speaking of ups and downs, it's funny how things turn out. I'm supposed to be on vacation for the next two weeks, but because we're short a few guys, I had to postpone it. Then what do you know, Bam! Your case lands flat on my desk. So, as I open it and begin to read, I'm saying to myself, 'Aaron Anderson?' The name rings such a familiar bell, and as I started gathering my thoughts, I remembered, 'Aaron Anderson!' The lefty who plays for 'The Spartans!' That's you, right?" Detective Aguilar began, his words weaving a connection between the unfolding family tragedy and Aaron's life on the baseball field.

Aaron and Tanashia felt a mix of relief and tension as Detective Aguilar recognized Aaron from his baseball career. They exchanged glances, silently sharing the weight of their recent ordeals. "Yes, officer, that's me."

Detective Aguilar chuckled, adding some tension. "Son, it's Detective. Now it all makes sense to me why you had such a rough game dealing with all of this. But yeah, my mind just never shuts off. So what happens? I get to thinking, 'Lefty?' So, I'd assume if you were being attacked by an assailant and chose to defend yourself with, let's say, a knife, more than likely you would use your left hand to swing a weapon like this, correct?"

Aaron remained quiet, contemplating how much he should reveal.

"Detective," Tanashia interjected, "We appreciate your understanding. It was self-defense, and this is not really a good time."

Detective Aguilar softly chuckled. "I'm just painting a picture, something that I tend to do when imagining a crime scene. Since everything happened in the act of self-defense, I wouldn't dare bring to life any of my ridiculous accusations. You two have been through more than enough, and I don't need that on my conscience. I'd like to actually enjoy my vacation. On that note, you guys take care and stay out of trouble." He proceeded to walk away.

"Oh, yeah, and 'Double-A,' I lost fifty on your game," Detective Aguilar added with a smirk.

"Yes, yes, Detective. Sorry about that, and thank you for your service," Aaron nervously responded.

Tracy rushed over, her concern evident. "Everything okay? What'd he say?" Tanashia reassured her, "Everything's okay."

"Good, 'cuz girl, I would have needed a padded room if I had lost you, too. I was already thinking of ways to bust you out," Tracy joked. "And what the heck is, 'Thank you for your service?' he a cop, not a soldier, fool. This boy needs some schooling."

The trio walked away, leaving behind the detective and the weight of the recent events. The outside air offered a slight reprieve, but the scars of the past were still fresh.

As they returned from the cemetery, Tracy broke the somber silence with an unexpected revelation.

"Hey, forgot to tell you that the job called back," Tracy said, her tone attempting to inject a bit of normalcy into the heavy atmosphere.

"What? You serious?" Tanashia's eyes widened with surprise.

"Yup. I told them you were in jail," Tracy grinned mischievously.

"Mom!" Tanashia exclaimed, a mix of exasperation and amusement in her voice.

"Just playing, you have orientation next Tuesday. I hope you went and bought some shoes already because you ain't wearing mine out," Tracy teased, glancing down at Tanashia's footwear.

Aaron softly chuckled, lightening the mood. Tanashia playfully rolled her eyes. "Please, don't encourage her."

*****

The day of Damon's burial arrived with heavy hearts and somber skies. Tracy and Tanashia, clad in black attire that mirrored their mourning souls, stood alongside the freshly dug grave, surrounded by an intimate group of friends and distant relatives who had come to pay their respects. The atmosphere was laden with sorrow, and the weight of the recent events lingered like an unspoken specter.

The air was thick with grief as the priest recited solemn prayers, seeking solace for the departed soul. Tanashia, her eyes swollen from countless tears, clutched a small bouquet of white lilies, Damon's favorite flowers. Tracy, her stoic demeanor barely concealing the anguish within, offered a silent prayer for her son. They took turns placing flowers on the casket, a final farewell to a life that had met a tragic end.

As Tanashia's mind raced with a flurry of thoughts and emotions, she found herself caught in a whirlwind of revelations and questions. The realization that her father and deceased brother shared a common liking for lilies sent a shiver down her spine, a haunting reminder of the interconnectedness of life and death. It was a bittersweet realization, a poignant reminder of the fragility of existence and the enduring ties that bound her family together, even in the face of loss. As she mulled over the significance of this shared affinity, Tanashia's thoughts turned to her mother and the mystery surrounding Damon's father. It was a topic that had always been shrouded in silence, a void of information that left Tanashia grasping for answers. She couldn't help but wonder about the secrets her mother held close, the buried truths that lay beneath the surface of their seemingly ordinary lives.

Subconsciously, Tanashia began to draw parallels between her father and Damon's unknown father, comparing their looks and personalities in a desperate attempt to unravel the enigma that surrounded Damon's origins. Could there be a connection between Damon's father and her own family? Was there a buried secret that her mother had kept hidden, even from her father, Cole? As these thoughts swirled in her mind, Tanashia felt a tumult of conflicting emotions threatening to overwhelm her. Grief, hurt, love, guilt, and curiosity battled for dominance within her, each emotion vying for her attention with a relentless intensity. Yet, despite the storm raging within her, Tanashia remained steadfast, her outward composure a shield against the turmoil brewing beneath the surface.

With a heavy heart, Tanashia made a conscious decision to keep her feelings in check, mindful of the pain it would cause her mother to unearth long-buried secrets and confront the ghosts of the past. She knew that her mother had already endured her fair share of suffering, and she was determined not to add to her burden. And so, with a steely resolve born of love and compassion, Tanashia pushed aside her own desires for answers, choosing instead to protect her family from further heartache. But deep down, beneath the facade of strength and composure, the questions continued to gnaw at her soul, a constant reminder of the tangled web of secrets that threatened to unravel their fragile peace.

In the midst of their sorrow, Tanashia had made a difficult decision – Aaron, still nursing wounds both physically and emotionally, would not attend Damon's funeral, even though he asked to. Tanashia couldn't bear the thought of exposing her younger brother to any potential harm. Suppressing the truth of what felt to be barbarous, Tanashia could not share with anyone, especially Kiki, that she was the one who brutally knifed Damon in order to save Aaron. Although guilt relentlessly chewed at her conscience, she knew the risk of the truth being exposed. Kiki's young pregnancy was already considered high-risk, which compelled her to stay in the hospital and not attend the heartbreaking service.

"Sorry, Aaron," Tanashia expressed with a heavy heart. "I just can't risk it. It's too dangerous right now, and you need to focus on healing."

Aaron, understanding the gravity of the situation, reluctantly accepted his sister's decision. The absence of his presence at the funeral left a palpable void, a missing link in the family chain that was now irreparably broken.

As the dirt-covered casket was lowered into the ground, the reality of Damon's death settled like an unshakable weight on the hearts of those present. The echoes of his troubled life and the circumstances that led to his demise reverberated in the minds of everyone gathered, leaving a poignant silence in their wake. The cemetery became a repository of memories, both bitter and sweet, as Tracy and Tanashia said their final goodbyes to a son and brother whose journey had ended in tragedy.

*****

As the funeral procession came to a somber close and the mourners dispersed, Tanashia, Tracy, and countless others were left to grapple with the aftermath of Damon's tragic end.

Three days later, they stood together once more, this time at Damon's graveside, silently paying their last respects amidst a sea of emotions too vast and complex to put into words. Meanwhile, in a stark interrogation room, Whiz sat with his public defender by his side, facing off against the formidable duo of the district attorney and a seasoned detective. The air crackled with tension as they delved into the murky depths of the case surrounding Damon's untimely demise, each side poised for a battle of wits and legal maneuvering.

As they walked away from the cemetery, life tentatively moved forward. The job offer symbolized a fresh start for Tanashia, a chance to rebuild amidst the ruins of the recent past. The healing process had just begun, and the sisters, alongside their mother, Tracy, faced an uncertain but hopeful future. The sterile walls of the interview room in the penitentiary confined Whiz, his eyes meeting the gaze of the detective, DA, and his own lawyer, a somber atmosphere enveloping the space.

Detective Aguilar, a man hardened by years in law enforcement, broke the silence. "Whiz, let's not dance around this. You're facing serious charges and murder, and it doesn't look good for you."

Whiz, leaning back in his chair, met the detective's gaze with an air of defiance. "Yeah, I know what I'm facing. But hear me out, Detective, I didn't do it. I didn't kill that guy." The DA, a stern figure in a tailored suit, interjected. "Whiz, the evidence is stacked against you. Your fingerprints were all over the murder weapon, and witnesses placed you at the scene. You need to give us something substantial to work with here."

Whiz exchanged glances with his lawyer, who offered a subtle nod of encouragement. Taking a deep breath, Whiz began his account. "Yo, check your man, cuz that's bullshit. Ain't no witness see me nowhere 'cuz I wasn't there. Ok, y'all might get me on prints, but I ain't kill him. And I ain't going down for somebody else's body." The detective leaned forward, his piercing gaze fixed on Whiz. "So, you're saying you were just an accomplice? That you had no intention of killing that man?"

Whiz denied the accusation. "No. I'm saying I had nothing to do with that. But I know who might have had something to do with it. Hear me out. I'm just trying to clear my name." The DA, skeptical but intrigued, pressed further. "And why should we believe you, Whiz? What evidence do you have that can do so?"

Whiz, now facing a critical moment, revealed what he knew. "I can give you their names, contacts, anything you need.

Bo and Turk orchestrated this whole thing. They wanted that guy gone, not me. Something to do with some stripper bitch. The old man was pissing away his pension, too."

The detective exchanged glances with the DA, considering Whiz's words carefully. "We'll need more than just names. Solid evidence, witnesses, something we can use to corroborate your story." Whiz, realizing the gravity of the situation, leaned forward. "I'll help you in any way I can, but you have to promise me one thing – protection. I can't survive in here if they find out I'm talking."

The room fell into contemplative silence as the wheels of justice began to turn, with Whiz caught in the intricate dance of truth and consequences.

Outside in the courtyard, Snatch and a few close friends sought solace in the comforting haze of smoke, their white t-shirts emblazoned with the image of their departed King of Kennedy Towers, Damon. Amidst shared memories and solemn tributes, they found a fleeting sense of camaraderie amidst the chaos of grief. Kennedy Towers loomed over the cityscape, a towering monument of urban life that served as the backdrop for the unfolding drama. Snatch and his entourage engaged in animated conversation with a group of women, the air thick with tension and the weight of unspoken words. The dimly lit corridors of the towers echoed with the hint of laughter and low murmurs, creating a hushed atmosphere prompted with anticipation.

Snatch, a figure with a reputation that preceded him, contemplated the possibility of escalating the conflict by taking retaliation on Whiz. Although he knew Whiz was not the one who killed his best friend, he understood that he'd still be alive if the beef between the two had not escalated. Plus, he could never harm Aaron, whose name on the street was the one who apparently killed Damon. Causing harm to Aaron is a direct attack on Tanashia, and at the end of the day, he has nothing but love for her. The tragedy had left its mark on the dynamics within the towers, and Snatch found himself at the center of a storm, both literal and metaphorical.

Meanwhile, just outside Kennedy Towers, a juvenile sought solace in the quiet confines of an alleyway. Sitting on a crate, the young figure toyed with the very gun that had recently been in the hands of Whiz. The weapon, a symbol of the volatile nature of life within the towers, was destined to play a pivotal role in the unfolding narrative.

As fate would have it, the police eventually discovered the gun. However, the accusations that followed were rendered unjustifiable due to a frustrating lack of evidence. The echoes of injustice reverberated through the towers, further fueling the underlying tensions that defined life within their walls.

Meanwhile, in the quiet sanctuary of his man-cave, Aaron found himself immersed in a deeply personal endeavor, creating a collage that served as a poignant tribute to his cherished memories. Baseball trophies gleamed alongside childhood photographs, capturing fleeting moments of innocence and joy shared with his parents, both past and present. Among them, a more recent image depicted Aaron and Tanashia, a testament to the enduring bonds and love that transcended the trials of time.

Amidst the bittersweet symphony of life and loss, inside the maternity ward, Kiki cradled a newborn baby boy, DJ, or Damon Jr., in her arms. Beside her stood Tanashia and Tracy, their hearts heavy with sorrow yet filled with a glimmer of hope for the future. In the innocent gaze of the newborn, they found solace amidst the storm, a reminder that life, in all its complexities, continued to unfold, even in the face of tragedy.

The sterile scent of antiseptic mixed with the sweet fragrance of new life as Shannon, Tanashia, and Tracy gathered around, forming a protective circle of support and sisterhood. The hospital room became a sanctuary of hope within the tumultuous landscape of Kennedy Towers. The newborn, innocent and unaware of the challenges that awaited him, symbolized the potential for change and renewal. The city outside the towers continued its ceaseless rhythm, oblivious to the microcosm of life that unfolded within Kennedy Towers. The characters, each with their unique stories, navigated the labyrinth of relationships, aspirations, and conflicts that defined their existence.